CW00869914

Directory of Publishing in Scotland 1993

Directory of Publishing in Scotland
1993

SCOTTISH PUBLISHERS ASSOCIATION

First published in 1988
Third edition published in 1993 by
SCOTTISH PUBLISHERS ASSOCIATION
Scottish Book Centre
137 Dundee Street
Edinburgh EH11 1BG

Copyright © Scottish Publishers Association 1993

All rights reserved. No part of this publication may be reproduced or transmitted in any form or by any means, electronic or mechanical, including photocopy, recording, or any information storage and retreival system, without permission in writing from the publisher. This book is sold subject to the condition that it shall not, by way of trade or otherwise, be lent, re-sold, hired out or otherwise circulated without the publisher's prior consent.

A CIP record for this book is available from the British Library.

ISBN: 0 9513912 1 6

Cover design by James Hutcheson
Printed and bound in Great Britain by The Cromwell Press

Contents

Introduction

Daily the Scottish Publishers Association (SPA) receives enquiries about books in Scotland, about the practicalities of an increasingly complex book business. What is needed is not simply a reference point for booksellers and publishers, but a source of information for authors and illustrators, designers, printers, consultants and freelance workers, as well as for the public in general. There has long been a number of specialist volumes in print, a selection of which is listed in the bibliography, but in compiling the first edition of the Directory of Publishing in Scotland in 1989, the SPA's priority was to assemble and highlight information for a Scottish readership. It proved to be useful and successful; this is its third, and much expanded, edition.

The Directory has been divided into two sections. The first part contains information on the Scottish literature, publishing, bookselling and library scenes, all of which receive support and encouragement from the Scottish Arts Council. This section also lists the current membership, publishers and bookshops, of the SPA and the Scottish Book Marketing Group (SBMG), respectively.

The second section of the book provides lists, alphabetically by category, of publishing services and support. The companies and individuals who appear here are those who replied to our call for information on their services in November 1992. It is hoped that those listed give a fair representation of services available in Scotland to authors, readers, publishers and booksellers - indeed anyone connected with or interested in the book trade.

It is hoped that from now on the Directory will be updated on an annual basis and the SPA would welcome any suggestions for future editions. The SPA needs up-to-date records in order to provide its services (described on the following pages) as it cannot work without your co-operation.

All information is correct at the time of going to press.

Acknowledgements

In compiling this volume we have been grateful for the help, encouragement and skills of a number of people.

Our thanks are due to Walter Cairns, Literature Director, Scottish Arts Council; Tessa Ransford, Director, Scottish Poetry Library; Robert Craig, Executive Secretary, Scottish Library Association; Shona Munro, Director, Edinburgh Book Festival; and to Lindsey Fraser and Kathryn Ross of Book Trust Scotland.

Our thanks must also go to all our contributors, especially those who have demonstrated their faith in this new project not only by submitting an entry but also by placing an advertisement. We hope that their services will be widely used.

SCOTTISH PUBLISHERS ASSOCIATION

Scottish Book Centre, 137 Dundee Street, Edinburgh EH11 1BG
Tel: 031 228 6866
Fax: 031 228 3220
Date established: 1974
Contacts: Lorraine Fannin (Director); Anna Fenge (Promotion and Marketing Manager); Helen Kemp (Administrator); Joanna Mattinson (SBMG); Beatrice Sayers
Services offered: Information, promotion and marketing services, advice and access to SPA reference and resource material. See **Aims** for a fuller description of SPA services to members.

Background:
Two hundred years separate the blue-chip days of Scottish publishing. Towards the end of the eighteenth century, and for the early years of the nineteenth, Edinburgh challenged London as the print capital of the world. In the space of a few decades some of the most illustrious names in publishing emerged and flourished, reflecting the intellectual optimism of the Enlightenment and Sir Walter Scott's phenomenal popularity at home and on the continent.

Firms like those of Archibald Constable (once called the Edinburgh University Press), and William Blackwood, whose influence through their respective periodicals, *Edinburgh Review* and *Blackwood's Magazine,* extended worldwide, were in the forefront of a publishing explosion. Others followed quickly at their heels; Thomas Nelson, A & C Black, Blackie & Son, W & R Chambers, William Collins, Oliver & Boyd, Bartholomew and T & T Clark all carved a niche for themselves in a competitive market-place, contributing to Edinburgh's boast of being a city built on beer, biscuits and books.

Publishing and printing were often carried out by the same company, but in more recent years this has become an obsolete practice. Booksellers were often publishers as well. But over the course of the nineteenth

9

century, the power centre gradually shifted back towards London. Some Scottish firms opened offices in the south, merged or expanded into conglomerates, Scottish in name only. By the 1960s several large Scottish publishers were still engaged in general publishing, though many more had fallen prey to the multinationals which now largely control what was once a family-dominated industry. But by the beginning of the 1970s, it was clear that some change was under way; new companies were springing up and Scottish writing was flourishing.

Around 40 small presses were extant in 1974, the same year that the Scottish Publishers Association was formed. The original group, known as the Scottish General Publishers Association, was formed by 12 publishers. The first chairman was Robin Lorimer, shortly followed by Norman Wilson, who worked with the other members to secure Arts Council support for this initiative - and it remains a continuing lifeline.

The SPA has now grown much more complex with a full programme of international marketing, services and promotions, but still provides the element of mutual help and advice which members share with each other, recognising a common purpose in a time of difficulty for the whole industry and combining all possible resources to work in bringing Scottish-published books to the attention of the reading public.

Aims:
The Scottish Publishers Association aims to help publishing concerns in Scotland to conduct their book publishing businesses in a professional manner, to market their output to the widest possible readership within Scotland, the UK and overseas and to encourage the development of a literary culture in Scotland.

A programme of activities is planned annually which provides a range of opportunity to all publishers, whatever their size, scope, speciality or geographical location. These activities are offered on a cooperative basis in order to save costs and administrative time. In outline they consist of: attendance at book fairs - home and abroad; marketing to bookshops, schools and libraries; publicity and advertising services; provision of professional training facilities in publishing skills, information resources and consultancy.

In addition the SPA implements research, develops projects and liaises with outside organisations which are considered to be of interest and benefit to the membership of the SPA, for example: Book House Training Centre, Book Trust and International Book Development.

The resources with which the SPA carries out these objectives include staff expertise, the premises and facilities of the Scottish Book Centre, financial assistance from the Scottish Arts Council, subscriptions from members and annual earnings from services offered. These resources are constantly developed to bring improved benefit to the membership.

Membership is open to all companies and organisations in Scotland who publish books for sale. Aspiring members should have published at least two books, whose authors should be other than the principals of the company. There should also be a commitment to a future publishing programme. Associate Membership is open to those concerns whose aims and aspirations are compatible with that of the SPA and who may be thought to derive benefit from the association, although they may not have fulfilled the membership criteria. Such members are not eligible for nomination to the Council of the SPA, this Council being elected annually by and from the membership.

The following services are offered to all members of the Association :
• A quarterly newsletter with marketing, trade fairs, employment, manuscripts, bookshop, overseas and general publishing information.
• Information, advice and access to the SPA reference and resource library.
• Access to services provided by International Book Development: helping with export initiative queries and providing an export newsletter for subscribing members, DTI information on British/Scottish

promotions abroad, and advertising opportunities overseas.

Other services offered are charged at low rates. They include:

• Advance information mailing (an advertisement in *Scottish Libraries Journal* and a mailing to all major bookshops, wholesalers, library suppliers, press and media contacts in Scotland, and to major media contacts in London).

• Printed insert in the export edition of *The Bookseller* in spring and autumn with a further 5,000 copies distributed via the SPA mailings to the UK book trade, media, school resource centres, universities, schools libraries, wholesalers, book clubs, library suppliers, all British Councils, and a number of overseas customers. The leaflet is used as promotional material at SPA displays, trade fairs and conferences.

• Mailing list labels from an extensive and regularly-updated database.

• Representation at book fairs in the UK and abroad. Members may display their books on the SPA stand, even if they do not attend the fair personally. The fairs attended are:

London Book Fair
Booksellers Association Conference
American Booksellers Association Convention
Frankfurt Book Fair
Moscow Book Fair (when appropriate)
The Edinburgh Book Festival
Scottish Library Association Conference
Schoolbook exhibitions
and many others.

• Promotional activities include joint advertising, press and media campaigns, book display facilities, Scottish Book Marketing Group promotions such as Scottish Book Fortnight and a summer tourist promotion. In addition, the publicist is available to assist members in planning individual press and publicity campaigns.

• Training in aspects of publishing; seminars on current publishing issues.

• Export sales consortium to facilitate overseas sales.

Full members

ACAIR LTD

7 James Street, Stornoway, Isle of Lewis PA87 2QA
Tel: 0851 70 3020
Fax: 0851 70 3294
ISBNs & Imprints: 0 86152
Company established: 1977
Titles in print: 158
Contacts: Joan Morrison (Editorial and Publicity); Donalda MacLeod (Sales Administration); Hugh Andrew (Sales) home address: Second Floor Left, 13 Roseneath Street, Edinburgh EH9 1JH
Type of books published: Children's books in Gaelic, general interest titles in Gaelic, Highlands and Islands history, biography, English.
Distributor: Acair Ltd

ATELIER BOOKS

4 Dundas Street, Edinburgh EH3 6HZ
Tel: 031 557 4050
Fax: 031 557 8382
ISBNs & Imprints: 0 951 and 1 873830
Company established: 1987
Titles in print: 4
Contacts: Patrick Bourne (Director); Roseanne Munro (Publishing Manager)
Type of books published: Books on art and artists.
Distributor: Atelier Books

AMAISING PUBLISHING HOUSE LTD, THE
PO Box, Musselburgh EH21 7UJ
Tel: 031 665 8237
Fax: 031 665 2582
ISBNs & Imprints: 1 87512
Company established: 1987
Titles in print: 24
Contacts: Katrena Allan (Managing Director, Accounts); Charles Watt (Production); Aileen Paterson (Editorial); Norma Rutherford (Sales and Marketing)
Type of books published: Children's illustrated.
Distributor: The Amaising Publishing House Ltd

ARGYLL PUBLISHING
Glendaruel, Argyll PA22 3AE
Tel: 0369 82229
Fax: 0369 82317
ISBNs & Imprints: 1 874640
Company established: July 1992
Titles in print: 8
Contact: Derek Rodger (Proprietor)
Type of books published: General titles including health, sport, biography, politics and fiction.
Distributor: Bookspeed, Edinburgh

ASSOCIATION FOR SCOTTISH LITERARY STUDIES
c/o Dept of English, University of Aberdeen, Aberdeen AB9 2UB
Tel: 0224 272634
ISBNs & Imprints: 0 948877
Company established: 1970
Titles in print: 26 plus journals
Contact: Dr David Hewitt (Editorial)
Type of books published: Editions of older literature, criticism, scholarship, contemporary literature.
Distributor: Nancy Robertson (Tel: 0224 872888)

BALNAIN BOOKS
Druim House, Lochloy Road, Nairn IV12 5LF
Tel: 0667 52940
Fax: 0667 55099
ISBNs & Imprints: 1 872557 and 0 9509792
Company established: 1983
Titles in print: 26
Contacts: Simon Fraser (Sales, Production); Sarah Fraser (Editorial, Publicity)
Type of books published: Fiction: general, contemporary, historical, Scottish, classic reprints; literature; non-fiction: horses, sport, holistic, biography.
Distributor: Balnain Books

B + W PUBLISHING
7 Sciennes, Edinburgh EH9 1NH
Tel: 031 667 6679
ISBNs & Imprints: 0 9515151 and 1 873631
Company established: 1990
Titles in print: 15
Contact: Campbell Brown
Type of books published: Fiction, memoirs, guide books, children's, reference.
Distributor: B + W Publishing

BAGPIPES OF CALEDONIA LTD (Printaway Ltd)
Lorn House, Links Gardens Lane, Leith, Edinburgh EH6 7JQ
Tel: 031 553 5503
Fax: 031 553 5550
ISBNs & Imprints: 0 9513230
Company established: 1985
Titles in print: 2
Contact: Jane Lawson
Type of books published: Piping and related material; music books.
Distributor: Bagpipes of Caledonia Ltd

BARTHOLOMEW/TIMES - a division of HarperCollins Publishers
Duncan Street, Edinburgh EH9 1TA
Tel: 031 667 9341
Telex: 728134
Fax: 031 662 4282
ISBNs & Imprints: 0 00447 Collins; 0 7230 Times Books; 0 7028
Bartholomew, Nicholson; 0 00360 Collins-Longman.
Company established: 1826
Titles in print: c700
Contacts: Barry Winkleman (Managing Director); Robin Orr
(Cartographic Director); Jeremy Westwood (Director of Rights and
Special Sales)
Type of books published: Maps, atlases, guide books.
Distributor: HarperCollins Publishers, PO Box, Glasgow G4 0NB

COLIN BAXTER PHOTOGRAPHY
Block 6, Caldwellside Industrial Estate, Lanark ML11 6SR
Tel: 0555 665022
Fax: 0555 664775
From June 1993: Grantown-on-Spey PH26 3NA
ISBNs & Imprints: 0 948661
Company established: 1982
Titles in print: 26
Contacts: Mike Rensner (Editorial and Publicity); Agnes Russell (Sales);
Colin Baxter (Managing Director)
Type of books published: High quality photographic books on land and
cityscape, natural history, biography, calendars and diaries. Also a
picture library featuring Scottish landscape, Yorkshire, Cotswolds, Lake
District, Bath, Charles Rennie Mackintosh, Iceland, France.
Distributor: (In Scotland) Colin Baxter Photography Ltd; (In England)
Bookpoint Ltd, 39 Milton Park, Abingdon, Oxon OX14 4TD Tel:
0235 835001

BIRLINN LTD
2FL, 13 Roseneath Street, Sciennes, Edinburgh EH9 1JH
Tel & Fax: 031 228 6189
ISBNs & Imprints: 1 874744
Company established: 1992
Titles in print: 4
Contact: Hugh Andrew (Editorial, Sales, Publicity)
Type of books published: Scottish classics & humour, local interest.
Distributor: Bookpoint Ltd, 39 Milton Park, Abingdon, Oxon OX14
4TD Tel: 0235 835001

BLACK ACE BOOKS
Ellemford Farmhouse, Duns, Berwickshire TD11 3SG
Tel: 03617 370
Fax: 03617 287
ISBNs & Imprints: 1 872988
Company established: 1992
Titles in print: 2
Contacts: Hunter Steele (Editorial, Production); Boo Wood (Sales, Publicity)
Type of books published: Non-fiction; new fiction, primarily by Scottish authors; paperback reprints of quality fiction.
Distributor: Black Ace Books

BROWN, SON & FERGUSON LTD
4-10 Darnley Street, Glasgow G41 2SD
Tel: 041 429 1234 (24hrs)
Fax: 041 420 1694
ISBNs & Imprints: 0 85174
Company established: c1850
Titles in print: 500+
Contacts: L Ingram-Brown (Joint Managing Director); D H Provan (Sales Manager)
Type of books published: Nautical and yachting, sea literature, ship's stationery, nautical magazine, drama, poetry, scout and guide books.
Distributor: Brown, Son & Ferguson Ltd

CANONGATE PRESS
14 Frederick Street, Edinburgh EH2 2HB
Tel: 031 220 3800
Fax: 031 220 3888   **Telex:** 72165 CANPUB
ISBNs & Imprints: 0 86241; Canongate Classics; Kelpies
Company established: 1990
Titles in print: 200
Contact: Stephanie Wolfe Murray (Publisher)
Type of books published: General interest, Scottish, fiction, poetry, art, history, biography, children's fiction.
Distributor: Bookpoint Ltd, 39 Milton Park, Abingdon, Oxon OX14 4TD Tel: 0235 835001

CENTRE FOR SCOTTISH STUDIES
University of Aberdeen, Old Brewery, King's College, Old Aberdeen AB9 2UB
Tel: 0224 272474
ISBNs & Imprints: 0 906265
Company established: 1972
Titles in print: 15
Contacts: John S Smith (Director and Editor of Pamphlets)
Type of books published: Scottish history and environmental history

W & R CHAMBERS LTD
43-45 Annandale Street, Edinburgh EH7 4AZ
Tel: 031 557 4571
Fax: 031 557 2936   **Telex:** 727967
ISBNs & Imprints: 0 550, 0245 and 086267
Company established: 1819   **Titles in print:** 566
Contacts: Chris McLaren (Sales and Marketing Director); Linda Orton (Marketing Manager); Dr T M Shepherd (Managing Director); John Clement (Chairman); Robert Allen (Editorial Director); Jack Osbourne (Production Director); Richard Drew (International Marketing Director)
Type of books published: English and bi-lingual dictionaries, English usage, modern languages, general reference, academic, Scottish interest.
Distributor: Chambers

CHAPMAN
4 Broughton Place, Edinburgh EH1 3RX
Tel: 031 557 2207
Fax: 031 556 9565
ISBNs & Imprints: 0 906772
Company established: 1970
Titles in print: 12
Contactss: Joy Hendry; Peter Cudmore (assistant)
Type of books published: Literary magazine, poetry, fiction. *Chapman*, Scotland's Quality Literary Magazine, is the mainstay of this small, dynamic publishing house. As well as the up-and-coming poets developed from the magazine, Chapman now publishes plays and short stories.
Distributor: Chapman

CHAPTER HOUSE LTD
26 Bothwell Street, Glasgow G2 6PA
Tel & Fax: 041 204 1285
ISBNs & Imprints: 0 948643
Company established: 1984
Titles in print: 9
Contacts: Nicholas Gray (Editorial); Marina Campbell (Sales, Publicity)
Type of books published: Religious.
Distributor: Mustard Seed (Scotland and Ireland), 38 Nethercliff Avenue, Netherlee, Glasgow G44 3UL Tel: 041 633 2075 and STL Distributors, PO Box 300, Kingstown Broadway, Carlisle CA3 0QS Tel: 0800 282728

CHURCHILL LIVINGSTONE
(Medical Division of Longman Group UK Ltd)
Robert Stevenson House, 1-3 Baxter's Place, Edinburgh EH1 3AF
Tel: 031 556 2424
Fax: 031 558 1278   **Telex:** 727511 LONGM G
ISBNs & Imprints: 0 443 and 0 272
Company established: 1724
Titles in print: 1500
Contacts: Andrew Stevenson (Managing Director); Peter Shepherd (Sales and Marketing Director); Sally Morris (Journals Director); John Richardson (Publishing Services Director); Peter Richardson (Publishing Director)
Type of books published: All areas of health science, including medicine, nursing, physiotherapy, dentistry, complementary medicine.
Distributor: Longman Group UK Ltd

EDINBURGH CITY LIBRARIES
Central Library, George IV Bridge, Edinburgh EH1 1EG
Tel: 031 225 5584
Fax: 031 225 8783
ISBNs & Imprints: 0 900353
Company established: 1890
Titles in print: 20
Contact: Norma Armstrong (Head of Information Services)
Type of books published: Books, booklets, prints, greetings cards.

EDINBURGH UNIVERSITY LIBRARY
George Square, Edinburgh EH8 9LJ
Tel: 031 650 3384
Fax: 031 667 9780   **Telex:** 727442 UNIVED G
ISBNs & Imprints: 0 907182
Company established: 1580
Titles in print: 22
Contacts: Miss Brenda E Moon; Mr Peter B Freshwater
Type of books published: Exhibition catalogues; finding lists; monographs based on Edinburgh University Library collections.

EDINBURGH UNIVERSITY PRESS and POLYGON
22 George Square, Edinburgh EH8 9LF
Tel: 031 650 4218
Fax: 031 662 0053
ISBNs & Imprints: 0 7486 and 0 85224 (EUP); 0 7486 and 0 904919 (Polygon)
Company established: 1948 (EUP); 1969 (Polygon)
Titles in print: 312 (EUP); 118 (Polygon)
Contacts: David Martin (Executive Chairman); Vivian Bone (Publisher and Editorial Director); Hazel Spalding (Customer Services); Ian Davidson (Production); Allan Woods (Business Manager); Alison Munro (Publicity); Marion Sinclair (Polygon Editorial)
Type of books published: EUP: Academic titles in Islamic studies, history, African studies, literature, archaeology, anthropology, philosophy, politics, sociology and women's studies. General titles in Scottish archaeology, Scottish history.
Polygon: new fiction and poetry, Determinations series on Scottish political culture, Scottish oral history.
Distributor: Edinburgh University Press Ltd

FINDHORN PRESS
The Park, Findhorn, Forres IV36 0TZ
Tel: 0309 690582
Fax: 0309 690933
ISBNs & Imprints: 0 905249 (Findhorn Press) and 0 906191 (Thule Press)
Company established: 1972
Titles in print: 24
Contacts: Karin Aubrey (Manager); Sandra Kramer (Editor)
Type of books published: New age, mostly originating from the Findhorn Foundation; also self development, ecological.
Distributor: Ashgrove Press, 4 Brassmill Centre, Brassmill Lane, Bath BA1 3JN

FLORIS BOOKS

15 Harrison Gardens, Edinburgh EH11 1SH
Tel: 031 337 2372
Fax: 031 346 7516
ISBNs & Imprints: 0 86315 and 0 903540
Company established: 1977
Titles in print: 193
Contacts: Christian Maclean (Chief Executive); Christopher Moore (Editorial); Alan Smart (Marketing); Christine McPhillips (Sales)
Type of books published: Celtic studies, Scottish studies, education, philosophy, mind, body and spirit, mythology, religion, science, craft and activity, children's.
Distributor for: Lindisfarne Press

FORTH NATURALIST AND HISTORIAN

The University of Stirling, Stirling FK9 4LA and 30 Dunmar Drive, Alloa FK10 2EH
Tel: 0259 215091
Fax: 0786 63000   **Telex:** 777557 STUNIV G
ISBNs & Imprints: 0 9506962 and 0 9514147   **ISSN:** 0309 7560
Company established: 1975
Titles in print: 10 plus 15 issues of annual journal plus 21 1890s maps
Contact: L Corbett, Honorary Editor/Secretary (Editorial, Sales, Publicity)
Type of books published: Environment, heritage, wildlife books and papers in annual Forth Naturalist and Historian and 1890s maps commissioned for central Scotland places from Godfrey of Newcastle.
Distributor: Forth Naturalist & Historian, University of Stirling

GEDDES & GROSSET LTD
David Dale House, New Lanark, Lanark ML11 9DB
Tel: 0555 665000
Fax: 0555 665694
ISBNs & Imprints: 1 85534
Company established: 1987
Titles in print: 90
Contacts: David Geddes, Ron Grosset, Mike Miller (Directors)
Type of books published: Reference, art, children's information and
paperback fiction.
Distributor: Grantham Book Services

GLASGOW CITY LIBRARIES PUBLICATIONS BOARD
The Mitchell Library, North Street, Glasgow G3 7DN
Tel: 041 221 7030
Fax: 041 204 4824 **Telex:** 778732 LIBGLW G
ISBNs & Imprints: 0 906169
Company established: 1980
Titles in print: 13 plus 1 as co-publisher and 20+ library bibliographies
Contacts: R McFarlane (Editorial); G Thomson (Sales and Publicity)
Type of books published: Mainly Glasgow interest or related to
material held in the Mitchell Library.
Distributor: The Mitchell Library at the above address

W GREEN, The Scottish Law Publisher
21 Alva Street, Edinburgh, EH2 4PS
Tel: 031 225 4879
Fax: 031 225 2104
ISBNs & Imprints: 0 414
Company established: 1734
Number of titles in print: 50
Contacts: Steven Mair (Managing Director); Gilly Michie (Publicity
and Promotions Manager)
Type of books published: Scots Law.
Distributor: International Thomson Publishing Services

HARPERCOLLINS PLC
Westerhill Road, Bishopbriggs, Glasgow G64 2QT
Tel: 041 772 3200
Fax: 041 762 0451   **Telex:** 778107 COLLINS G
ISBNs & Imprints: 0 00
Company established: 1819
Titles in print: 10,000
Contacts: Caroline McCreath (Publishing Director, Travel and General Reference); David Taylor (Sales); Nick Wells (Marketing)
Type of books published: General fiction, non-fiction, biography, history, dictionaries and reference, children's, religious, including bibles, educational, sport, travel, home and leisure, cartographic.
Distributor: HarperCollins

HMSO SCOTLAND
South Gyle Crescent, Edinburgh EH12 9EB
Tel: 031 479 9000
Fax: 031 479 3300
ISBNs & Imprints: 0 10 and 0 11
Company established: 1911
Titles in print: 30,000
Contact: Dr Susan Hemmings (Editorial, Sales, Publicity and Distribution)
Type of books published: Parliamentary and governmental material, historical, tourist guide books, exhibition catalogues, Scottish interest publications.
Distributor: HMSO

LYLE PUBLICATIONS LTD

Glenmayne, Galashiels, Selkirkshire TD1 3NR
Tel: 0896 2005
Fax: 0896 4696
ISBNs & Imprints: 0 86248
Company established: 1969
Titles in print: 16
Contacts: Tony Curtis (Editorial); John Masters (Sales); Eelin McIvor (Publicity); Donna Rutherford (Distribution)
Type of books published: Price guides to antiques, collectibles and paintings.
Distributor: Lyle Publications

MAINSTREAM PUBLISHING

7 Albany Street, Edinburgh EH1 3UG
Tel: 031 557 2959
Fax: 031 556 8720
ISBNs & Imprints: 1 85158 and 0 906391
Company established: 1978
Titles in print: c300
Contacts: Bill Campbell (Editorial Director); Peter MacKenzie (Financial Director); Raymond Cowie (Sales Manager); Andrew Young (Publicity Manager)
Type of books published: General non-fiction, fiction, biography, autobiography, art, photography, health, sport.
Distributor: Mainstream Publishing

MERCAT PRESS
at James Thin Ltd, 53-59 South Bridge, Edinburgh EH1 1YS
Tel: 031 556 6743
Fax: 031 557 8149
ISBNs & Imprints: 0 901824 and 1 873644; 0 800 (ex-Aberdeen University Press numbers)
Date established: 1970
Titles in print: 350
Contacts: Tom Johnstone; Sean Costello
Type of books published: Scottish interest general and academic books.
Distributor: From the above address

MERCHISTON PUBLISHING
Dept of Print Media, Publishing and Communication, Napier University, Colinton Road, Edinburgh EH10 5DT
Tel: 031 444 2266 ext 2569
Fax: 031 452 8532
ISBNs & Imprints: 0 9511
Company established: 1988
Titles in print: 5
Contact: Dr Alistair McCleery
Type of books published: Merchiston Publishing provides a realistic working environment for students on BA Publishing. It specialises in books on Scottish publishing and publishing in general.
Distributor: Merchiston Publishing

NATIONAL GALLERIES OF SCOTLAND
Belford Road, Edinburgh EH4 3DR
Tel: 031 556 8921
Fax: 031 315 2963
ISBNs & Imprints: 0 903148 and 0 903598
Titles in print: 57
Contact: Janis Adams (Editorial, Sales, Publicity and Distribution)
Type of books published: Art/photography books and catalogues.
Distributor: Lund Humphries

NATIONAL LIBRARY OF SCOTLAND
George IV Bridge, Edinburgh EH1 1EW
Tel: 031 226 4531 and 031 459 4531
Fax: 031 220 6662 **Telex:** 72638 NLSEDI G
ISBNs & Imprints: 0 90222 and 1 87211
Company established: 1925
Titles in print: 50
Contacts: Publications Officer (Editorial and Publicity); Publications Sales (Sales and Distribution)
Type of books published: Bibliographies, facsimiles, catalogues, literary and historical books.
Distributor: National Library of Scotland

NATIONAL MUSEUMS OF SCOTLAND
Chambers Street, Edinburgh EH1 1JF
Tel: 031 225 7534
Fax: 031 220 4819
ISBNs & Imprints: 0 948636; Trustees of the National Museums of Scotland
Company established: 1985 (under present name)
Titles in print: 41
Contacts: Jenni Calder (Museum Editor); Liz Robertson (Production)
Type of books published: Trade, scholarly, children's books in the following subjects: history, art, archaeology, science, technology, ethnography, geology, natural history.
Distributor: (In Scotland) National Museums of Scotland trading company; Gazelle Book Services Ltd (UK except Scotland, Europe)

NEIL WILSON PUBLISHING LTD

Suite 309, The Pentagon Centre, 36 Washington St, Glasgow G3 8AZ
Tel: 041 221 1117
Fax: 041 221 5363
ISBNs & Imprints: 1 897784
Company established: 1992
Titles in print: 9
Contacts: Neil Wilson
Type of books published: Whisky and beer, hillwalking, sport, Scottish history, biography, humour.
Distributor: Exel Logistics Media Services, 3 Sheldon Way, Larkfield, Maidstone ME20 6SE Tel: 0622 882000 Fax: 0622 718036

THOMAS NELSON AND SONS LTD

Bishopbriggs, Glasgow G64 2NZ
Tel: 041 772 2311
Fax: 041 762 0897
ISBNs & Imprints: 0 17   Nelson Blackie
Company established: 1798   **Titles in print:** 6,000
Contacts: David McCormick (Editorial); Heather Moore (Production); Ian Birchenough (Sales/Publicity)
Type of books published: Educational textbooks and resources for every key area of the school curriculum.
Distributor: International Thomson Publishing Services, Cheriton House, North Way, Andover, Hants SP10 5BE Tel: 0264 332424

NEW IONA PRESS, THE

7 Drynie Terrace, Inverness IV2 4UP
Tel: 0463 242384
ISBNs & Imprints: 0 9516283
Company established: 1990
Titles in print: 3
Contact: Mairi MacArthur (Director)
Type of books published: Local and natural history of the Hebrides, with special emphasis on the island of Iona.
Distributor: The New Iona Press

PENTLAND PRESS LTD
3 Regal Lane, Soham, Ely, Cambridge CB7 5BA
Tel: 0353 723359
ISBNs & Imprints: 0 946270
Company established: 1984
Titles in print: 130
Contacts: Nicholas Law (Chairman); Anthony Phillips (Editorial); Libby Jennings (Sales); Daniel Russell (Production); Rosemary Rudd (Publicity and Promotion)
Type of books published: Autobiographical, historical, general fiction, religious.
Distributor: Pentland Press Ltd

POLYGON
see under Edinburgh University Press

RAMSAY HEAD PRESS, THE
15 Gloucester Place, Edinburgh EH3 6EE
Tel: 031 225 5646
ISBNs & Imprints: 0 902859 and 1 873921
Company established: 1968
Titles in print: 32
Contacts: Christine and Conrad Wilson (Editorial); Christine Wilson (Sales, Advertising); M K Young (Accounts)
Type of books published: Scottish interest, autobiography, biography, fiction, poetry, academic, art and architecture, language books and literary criticism.
Distributor: The Ramsay Head Press

ROYAL INCORPORATION OF ARCHITECTS IN SCOTLAND (RIAS)
15 Rutland Square, Edinburgh EH1 2BE
Tel: 031 229 7545
Fax: 031 228 2188
ISBNs & Imprints: 1873190 RIAS; 09501462 and 070730 joint with Scottish Academic Press; 185158 joint with Mainstream
Company established: c1890
Titles in print: 16
Contacts: Joyce Allan (Commercial Director); Helen Leng (Publishing Manager)
Type of books published: Illustrated architectural guides.
Distributor: RIAS Distribution

SAINT ANDREW PRESS
121 George Street, Edinburgh EH2 4YN
Tel: 031 225 5722
Fax: 031 220 3113
ISBNs & Imprints: 0 7152 (Saint Andrew Press); 0 86153 (Church of Scotland)
Company established: 1954
Titles in print: 151
Contacts: Lesley A Taylor (Publishing Manager); Derek Auld (Sales and Production Manager); Ian Dunnet (Distribution); Isabel Cunningham (Invoicing)
Type of books published: Church of Scotland related titles and books for the wider Christian market. Local interest and some general.
Distributor: Saint Andrew Press

SALTIRE SOCIETY, THE
9 Fountain Close, 22 High Street, Edinburgh EH1 1TF
Tel: 031 556 1836
Fax: 031 557 1675
ISBNs & Imprints: 0 85411 0, 0 863340 and 0 904265; The Saltire Society, Lines Review Editions
Society established: 1936
Titles in print: 39
Contacts: Hugh Andrew (Marketing/Sales) 2FL, 13 Roseneath Street, Edinburgh EH9 1JH Tel/fax: 031 228 6189; Thorbjorn Campbell (Publications Officer) Gleniffer Place, 3 Miller Road, Ayr KA7 2AX Tel/fax: 0292 262359
Type of books published: History, law, current affairs, poetry, biography, Scottish interest.
Distributor: John Donald Distribution Services, 138 St Stephen Street, Edinburgh EH3 5AA Tel: 031 652 0823 Fax: 031 220 0567

SCOTTISH COUNCIL FOR RESEARCH IN EDUCATION
15 St John Street, Edinburgh EH8 8JR
Tel: 031 557 2944
Fax: 031 556 9454
ISBNs & Imprints: 0 947833 and 1 873303
Company established: 1928
Titles in print: 101
Contacts: Dave Gilhooly (Sales, Distribution and Marketing); Rosemary Wake (Editorial); Joyce Corrigan (Sales enquiries)
Type of books published: Educational, research.
Distributor: Scottish Council for Research in Education

SCOTTISH LIBRARY ASSOCIATION

Motherwell Business Centre, 124/6 Coursington Road, Motherwell ML1 1PW
Tel: 0698 252526/252057
Fax: 0698 252057
ISBNs & Imprints: 0 900649
Company established: 1908
Titles in print: 12
Contact: Honorary Publications Officer, Alan Reid, c/o Midlothian District Council, Library HQ, 7 Station Road, Roslin, Midlothian EH25 9PF
Type of books published: Librarianship, bibliographies, Scottish interest, local and national history.
Distributor: Scottish Library Association

SHETLAND TIMES LTD

Prince Alfred Street, Lerwick, Shetland ZE1 0EP
Tel: 0595 3622
Fax: 0595 4637
ISBNs & Imprints: 0 900662 - Shetland Times Ltd
Company established: 1872
Titles in print: 30
Contacts: Robert Wishart (Managing Director); Beatrice Nisbet (Publications Manager)
Type of books published: Local interest.
Distributor: The Shetland Times Bookshop, 71-79 Commercial Street, Lerwick, Shetland ZE1 0AJ

SOCIETY OF WEST HIGHLAND AND ISLAND HISTORICAL RESEARCH LTD

Breacachadh Castle, Isle of Coll, Argyll PA78 6TB
Tel: 08793 444
Fax: 08793 357 **Telex:** 777325 PROJECT G
ISBNs & Imprints: 0 906366
Company established: 1972
Titles in print: 9
Contact: Nicholas MacLean-Bristol (Editorial, Sales, Publicity and Distribution)
Type of books published: Historical related to West Highlands and Islands.
Distributor: Society of West Highland and Island Research Ltd

SPA BOOKS LTD

PO Box 47, Stevenage, Herts SG2 8UH
Tel: 0462 482812
Fax: 0438 310104
ISBNs & Imprints: 0 907590 SPA Books; 1 871048 Strong Oak Press
Company established: 1980
Titles in print: 150
Contact: Steven Apps (Editorial, Production, Sales/Publicity)
Type of books published: Military history, Scottish interest, publishing skills, history, biography.
Distributor: SPA Books Ltd

RICHARD STENLAKE

1 Overdale Street, Langside, Glasgow G42 9PZ
Tel: 041 632 2304
ISBNs & Imprints: 1 872074
Company established: 1990
Titles in print: 24
Contacts: Richard Stenlake; Campbell McCutcheon
Type of books published: Local history, industrial history, transport history, postcard-related, Scottish interest.
Distributor: Richard Stenlake/Stenlake & McCourt

TARRAGON PRESS
Moss Park, Ravenstone, Whithorn DG8 8DR
Tel: 098 885 368
Fax: 098 885 304
ISBNs & Imprints: 1 870781
Company established: 1987
Titles in print: 3
Contact: David Sumner (Director)
Type of books published: Science and medicine.
Distributor: Lavis Marketing, Oxford

DAVID ST JOHN THOMAS PUBLISHER
PO Box 4, Nairn IV12 4HU
Tel: 0667 54441
Fax: 0667 54401
ISBNs & Imprints: 0 946537 David St John Thomas Publisher; 0 946537 Writers News Library of Writing
Company established: 1989
Titles in print: 56
Contacts: Jo Royle (Editorial); Grant Shipcott (Production); Sharon Compton (Sales/Publicity)
Type of books published: Railway, transport history, writing, Scottish interest.
Distributor: Bookpoint Ltd, 39 Milton Park, Abingdon, Oxon OX14 4TD Tel: 0235 835001

UNIT FOR THE STUDY OF GOVERNMENT IN SCOTLAND

31 Buccleuch Place, Edinburgh EH8 9JT
Tel: 031 650 4458
ISSN: 0966 0356
Company established: 1976
Titles in print: 6
Contacts: Dr Lindsay Paterson (Editorial); Mrs Helen Ramm (Production and Sales/Publicity)
Type of books published: Research and debate on social, political, economic and cultural topics which might be of particular interest to Scotland, also similarly placed small nations/regions throughout Europe and beyond.
Distributor: Unit for the Study of Government in Scotland

WHIGMALEERIE STORY CASSETTES

Main Street, Balerno, Edinburgh EH14 7EQ
Tel: 031 449 5893
ISBNs & Imprints: 1 870342
Company established: 1985
Titles in print: 27 cassettes; 1 book
Contacts: Pam Wardell (Editorial); Moira Small (Sales and Publicity)
Type of cassettes: Scottish, children's.
Distributor: Whigmaleerie/Lomond Books

WHITE COCKADE PUBLISHING
Wendlebury House, Church Lane, Wendlebury, Oxon OX6 8PN
Tel: 0869 241450
Fax: 0869 248195
ISBNs & Imprints: 0 9513124 and 1 873487
Company established: 1988
Titles in print: 5
Contact: Perilla Kinchin (Director)
Type of books published: Books for the general and specialist reader in architecture, design, art and social history (especially Scottish).
Distributor: White Cockade Publishing

WHITTLES PUBLISHING
Roseleigh House, Harbour Rd, Latheronwheel, Caithness KW5 6DW
Tel & Fax: 05934 240
ISBNs & Imprints: 1 870325
Company established: 1986
Titles in print: 15
Contacts: Dr Keith Whittles (Editorial, Sales and Publicity); Sue Steven (Editorial, Sales)
Type of books published: Science (primarily geology, geochemistry and petroleum geology); civil engineering and surveying; Scottish interest.
Distributor: Whittles Publishing

WILD GOOSE PUBLICATIONS
The Iona Community, Pearce Institute, 840 Govan Road, Glasgow G51 3UU
Tel: 041 445 4561
Fax: 041 445 4295
ISBNs & Imprints: 0 947988
Company established: 1985
Titles in print: 34
Contact: Susi Cormack
Type of books published: Religious, especially drama, music (books and tapes) and other worship resources.
Distributor: Wild Goose Publications

Associate Members

BOOK TRUST SCOTLAND

Scottish Book Centre, 137 Dundee Street, Edinburgh EH11 1BG
Tel: 031 229 3663
Fax: 031 228 4293
ISBNs & Imprints: 0 85353
Company established: 1961
Titles in print: 3
Contacts: Lindsey Fraser (Executive Director); Kathryn Ross (Depute Executive Director)
Type of books published: Bibliographies, posters, *In Brief* series, book guides for children and adults. Currently in print *The Directory of Children's Writers from Scotland, Books for Babies* (with exhibition), *How Things Work* (with exhibition).
Distributor: Book Trust Scotland

GAELIC BOOKS COUNCIL, THE

Department of Celtic, University of Glasgow, Glasgow G12 8QQ
Tel: 041 330 5190
ISBNs & Imprints: 0 9512810
Company established: 1968
Titles in print: 1
Contact: Ian MacDonald
Type of books published: Catalogues and book news magazines.
Distributor: The Gaelic Books Council

KINMOR MUSIC
Shillinghill, Temple, Midlothian EH23 4SH
Tel: 0875 30 328
Fax: 0875 30 392
ISBNs & Imprints: 0 9511204
Titles in print: 4
Contacts: Robin Morton (Editorial, Production); Sarah Stott (Sales,Publicity)
Type of books published: Harp tunes arranged by Alison Kinnaird; Harp tutor with accompanying cassette; songs and tunes written by or arranged by Battlefield Band; history of the harp in Scotland.
Distributor: Temple Records, Shillinghill, Temple EH23 4SH

SCOTTISH OFFICE, THE
The Scottish Office Library, Publication Sales, Rm 1/44, New St Andrew's House, Edinburgh EH1 3TG
Tel: 031 244 4796
Fax: 031 244 4785/4786   **Telex:** 727301 NSCOTO G
ISBNs & Imprints: 0 74800   **Company established:** 1939
Titles in print: 950
Contact: Assistant Librarian (Official Publications)
Type of books published: Scottish Office publications not published by HMSO, such as official reports, central research unit papers, statistical publications - including "Scottish Abstract of Statistics".
Distributor: The Scottish Office Library, Edinburgh

STRAIGHT LINE PUBLISHING LTD
6 Kylepark Avenue, Uddingston G71 7DF
Tel: 0698 814357
Fax: 0698 854448
Company established: 1989
Titles in print: 4
Contacts: F Docherty (Production); P Bellew (Sales/Publicity)
Type of books published: Specialist facts books, education dept. projects, annual reports, *Institute Quarterly*.
Distribution: Straight Line Publishing Ltd

Non-Member Publishers

JOHN DONALD PUBLISHERS
138 St Stephen Street, Edinburgh EH3 5AA
Tel: 031 225 1146
Fax: 031 220 0567
ISBNs & Imprints: 0 85976
Company established: 1973
Titles in print: 162
Contacts: Gordon Angus (Sales Promotion and Distribution); D L Morrison (Production); Russell Walker (Editorial)
Type of books published: Academic books on history, archaeology and the social sciences; Scottish local history; general books on Scotland; *Discovering* series on Scotland and England.
Distributor: John Donald Distribution

ROBERT GIBSON & SONS
17 Fitzroy Place, Glasgow G3 7SF
Tel: 041 248 5674
Fax: 041 221 8219
ISBNs & Imprints: 0 7169
Company established: 1862
Titles in print: Around 200
Contacts: Mrs Pinkerton (Sales); Mr Crawford (Production); Mr Gibson (Editorial)
Type of books published: Educational. Agents for SEB.
Distributor: Robert Gibson & Sons

T & T CLARK LTD
59 George Street, Edinburgh EH2 2LQ
Tel: 031 225 4703
Fax: 031 220 4260
ISBNs & Imprints: 0 567
Company established: 1821
Titles in print: Over 400
Contacts: Callum Fisken (Sales); Elizabeth Nicol (Production); Geoffrey Green (Editorial)
Type of books published: Academic and professional books and periodicals in theology, philosophy and law.
Distributor: T & T Clark

TETRAHEDRON BOOKS
30 Birch Crescent, Blairgowrie, Perthshire PH10 6TS
Company established: 1992
Contact: Peter Mackie (Sales, Editorial and Production)
Type of books published: Books on the problems of young people, and first hand accounts of experiences of ex-psychiatric patients; also some poetry.

THISTLE PRESS
West Bank, Western Road, Insch, Aberdeenshire AB52 6JR
Tel: 0464 21053
Company established: 1992
Titles in print: 1
Contacts: Angela or Keith Nicholson
Type of books published: Scottish regional travel guides which emphasise aspects of local history, archaeology and geology. Visitor attractions such as sports facilities and craft shops are also included.
Distributor: Thistle Press

Scottish Book Marketing Group

SCOTTISH BOOK MARKETING GROUP
Scottish Book Centre, 137 Dundee Street, Edinburgh EH11 1BG
Tel: 031 228 6866
Fax: 031 228 3220
Date established: 1986
Contacts: Joanna Mattinson; Anna Fenge
Services offered: Scottish Book Fortnight; fortnightly, quarterly and annual Scottish Bestseller Lists; spring/summer promotion; information and advisory service; access to reference and resource material; purpose-built venue for meetings, training courses or conferences.
Description of services: See below.

The Scottish Book Marketing Group is an unique venture set up by the Scottish Publishers Association and the Booksellers Association (Scottish branch). Its aims are to promote Scottish books through Scottish bookshops, with the assistance of participating libraries, and to create a wider public awareness of their quality, range and availability - as well as to provide a platform for Scottish authors. Currently SBMG membership consists of over 40 bookseller members, including independents, chains and wholesalers, who are listed on the following pages.

To date SBMG activities have been concerned with four major initiatives:
• A fortnightly Bestseller List for Scotland, which appears regularly in the press. A list which highlights bestsellers of the year in Scotland is also compiled and quarterly lists, covering various topics, are currently being introduced.
• A nationwide autumn promotion, Scottish Book Fortnight. Held annually in October/November, the Book Fortnight promotes Scottish titles with a full meet-the-author events programme and displays throughout the country. (Dates for the 1993 promotion are Saturday 16 to Saturday 30 October.)
• A spring/summer books promotion aimed at the large Scottish tourist market.
• An information and advisory service for all members.

Staff and members are keen to develop and strengthen the activities programme of the Group and to encourage new members. As the organisation is based in the recently opened Scottish Book Centre all members have access to the fully equipped meeting room for conference or training purposes.

The SBMG is run by a committee comprised equally of bookseller and publisher members, plus a Scottish library and author representative. The Group is administered by the Scottish Publishers Association and has the support of the SPA staff and services.

S B M G Bookshop Members

Aberdeen

BISSETS
12-14 Upperkirkgate, Aberdeen AB9 1BG
Tel: 0224 644528
Fax: 0224 630032
Contacts: Mr Anthony F Schmitz (Manager); Miss Joyce Gordon (Assistant Manager)
Subject specialisations: HMSO database interrogation and ordering, bibliographic searching and supply.

DILLONS THE BOOKSTORE
269-271 Union Street, Aberdeen AB1 2BR
Tel: 0224 210161
Fax: 0224 211808
Contact: Richard Hills (Manager)

WATERSTONE'S BOOKSELLERS
236 Union Street, Aberdeen AB1 1TN
Tel: 0224 571655
Contacts: John Green (Manager); Fiona Watson (Assistant Manager)

Aviemore

MELVEN'S BOOKSHOP
The Freedom Inn Hotel Complex, Aviemore PH22 1PF
Tel: 0479 810797
Contact: Ann Stewart (Manager)

Ayr

JAMES THIN
15 Sandgate, Ayr KA7 1BG
Tel: 0292 611011
Contacts: Phyllis Weir (Manager); Mrs Dalling (Assistant Manager)
Subject specialisations: Scottish and local interest.

Bowmore

C & E ROY
The Celtic House, Bowmore, Isle of Islay, Argyll PA43 7LD
Tel: 049 681 304
Fax: 049 681 647
Contact: Colin P Roy (Manager)
Subject specialisations: Celtic, Scottish and local interest.

Dornoch

THE DORNOCH BOOKSHOP
High Street, Dornoch, Sutherland IV25 3SH
Tel: 0862 810165
Fax: 0862 810197
Contact: Richard Butterworth (Proprietor)
Subject specialisations: Scotland (the Highlands in particular), golf and children's books.

Dumfries

THE BOOK PLACE
T C Farries & Co (Library Supplier), Irongray Road, Lochside, Dumfries DG2 0LH
Tel: 0387 720755
Fax: 0387 721105
Contacts: Robert Hawthorn (Manager); Neill Ross (Stock Manager)

JAMES THIN
18-26 Church Crescent, Dumfries DG1 1DQ
Tel: 0387 54288
Contact: Lorraine McLean (Manager)

Dundee

JOHN SMITH & SON (GLASGOW) LTD
University Bookshop, Students' Association, Airlie Place, Dundee DD1 4HN
Tel: 0382 202790
Contact: Mrs Ann Leslie (Manager)

JAMES THIN
7-8 High Street, Dundee DD1 1SS
Tel: 0382 23999
Fax: 0382 202963
Contact: Gordon Dow (Manager)
Subject specialisations: General, academic, local interest and Scottish titles.

WATERSTONE'S BOOKSELLERS
35 Commercial Street, Dundee DD1 3DG
Tel: 0382 200322
Contacts: Trevor Barton (Manager); Trevor Corfield (Events)
Subject specialisations: Scottish fiction, Scottish travel, science fiction, Scottish law and children's books.

Dunoon

BOOKPOINT
147-149 Argyll Street, Dunoon PA23 7DD
Tel: 0369 2377
Contact: Fiona Roy (Manager)
Subject specialisations: Wide selection of Scottish books - fiction and non-fiction.

Edinburgh

BODY & SOUL
52 Hamilton Place, Edinburgh EH3 5AX
Tel: 031 226 3066
Contact: Donald Busby (Manager)
Subject specialisations: Mind, body and spirit.

BOOKSPEED (Wholesaler)
48 Hamilton Place, Edinburgh EH3 5AX
Tel: 031 225 4950
Fax: 031 220 6515
Contacts: Kingsley Dawson (Director); Annie Rhodes (Director)
Subject specialisations: Scottish, general and children's books.

KAY'S BOOKSHOP
390 Morningside Road, Edinburgh EH10 5HX
Tel: 031 447 1265
Contact: Ian Taylor (Proprietor)

THE MUSEUM SHOP
National Museums of Scotland, Chambers Street, Edinburgh EH1 1JF
Tel: 031 225 7534 ext 128
Fax: 031 220 4819
Contact: Madge Maclean (Shop Manager)
Subject specialisations: Books, gifts, toys, stationery, postcards and posters relating to the collections.

JAMES THIN
57 George Street, Edinburgh EH2 2JQ
Tel: 031 225 4495
Fax: 031 225 9626
Contacts: Malcolm Gibson (Manager); Judith Paterson; Lorna Dixon (Events)
Subject specialisations: Fiction, reference, maps, travel, business, cookery and children's books.

JAMES THIN
53-59 South Bridge, Edinburgh EH1 1YS
Tel: 031 556 6743
Fax: 031 557 8149
Contacts: Ainslie Thin (Chairman); James Shaw (Bookshop Manager);
Mrs P Britton (Events)
Subject specialisations: General and academic books, also antiquarian
and secondhand.

JAMES THIN
Unit 1, Waverley Shopping Centre, Edinburgh EH1 1BQ
Tel: 031 557 1378
Contact: Clare Blackstock (Manager)

WATERSTONE'S BOOKSELLERS
83 George Street, Edinburgh EH2 3ES
Tel: 031 225 3436
Fax: 031 226 4548
Contacts: Maggie Lennon (Manager); Duncan Furness (Assistant
Manager)

WATERSTONE'S BOOKSELLERS
13-14 Princes Street, Edinburgh EH2 2AN
Tel: 031 556 3034
Fax: 031 557 8801
Contacts: Jerry Welch (Manager); Iain McFarlane (Assistant Manager);
Ian Docherty (Events)
Subject specialisations: Scottish interest, fiction, computing, children's
books, cookery, travel, sport and gender issues.

WATERSTONE'S BOOKSELLERS
West End Branch, 128 Princes Street, Edinburgh EH2 4AD
Tel: 031 226 2666
Fax: 031 226 4689
Contacts: Matthew Perren (Manager); Douglas McCabe (Events)
Subject specialisations: Scottish, academic, reference & language books.

Fraserburgh

JOHN TRAIL LTD
9 Mid Street, Fraserburgh AB4 5AJ
Tel: 0346 23307
Fax: 0346 23307
Contacts: Mrs Maitland (Proprietor); Mrs Anne Lomberg (Bookshop Manager)
Subject specialisations: Scottish, local interest and children's books.

Glasgow

ALBANY BOOK COMPANY LTD (Library and School Supplier)
30 Clydeholm Road, Glasgow G14 0BJ
Tel: 041 954 2271
Fax: 041 958 1198
Contacts: Jonathan Ridge (Sales and Marketing Director); Jane Churchill (Events)
Subject specialisations: Books, tapes, videos and school textbooks.

DILLONS THE BOOKSTORE
174-176 Argyle Street, Glasgow G2 8AH
Tel: 041 248 4814
Fax: 041 248 4622
Contact: Andrew Mitchell (Manager)

MILNGAVIE BOOKSHOP
37 Douglas Street, Milngavie, Glasgow G62 6PE
Tel: 041 956 4752
Fax: 041 956 4819
Contact: Terry Lane (Manager)

PICKERING & INGLIS
26 Bothwell Street, Glasgow G2 6PA
Tel: 041 221 8913
Fax: 041 204 1285
Contact: Nicholas Gray (Manager)
Subject specialisations: Scottish, children's, Christian books and bibles.

JOHN SMITH & SON (GLASGOW) LTD
252 Byres Road, Glasgow G12 8SH
Tel: 041 334 2769
Contact: Alison Stroak (Manager)
Subject specialisations: Paperbacks, Scottish and children's books plus an unusual music section.

JOHN SMITH & SON (GLASGOW) LTD
57 St Vincent Street, Glasgow G2 5TB
Tel: 041 221 7472
Fax: 041 248 4412
Contacts: Robert Clow (Managing Director); Willie Anderson (Assistant Managing Director); Moira Macmillan (Manager)
Subject specialisations: Six floors of bookselling, specialising in all subjects.

W H SMITH
53 Argyle Street, Glasgow G2 8AH
Tel: 041 221 6061
Contacts: Lynn Bolland (Bookshop Manager); John Kelly (Events)
Subject specialisations: Local interest, education, nursing and children's books.

WATERSTONE'S BOOKSELLERS
45-50 Princes Square, Glasgow G1 3JN
Tel: 041 221 9650
Contacts: Robert Kinnear (Manager); Jo Ferguson (Events)
Subject specialisations: Scottish, history, art, travel, cookery, crafts, architecture and biography.

WATERSTONE'S BOOKSELLERS
132 Union Street, Glasgow G1 3QQ
Tel: 041 221 0890
Fax: 041 221 4067
Contacts: Claire Edwards (Manager); Tim Batten (Events)

Greenock

BOOKPOINT
93 West Blackhall Street, Greenock, Renfrewshire PA15 1XP
Tel & Fax: 0475 85050
Contact: Catherine Turnbull (Manager)

Inverness

DILLONS THE BOOKSTORE
12-14 Inglis Street, Inverness IV1 1HN
Tel: 0463 237495
Contact: Rosemary Stewart (Manager)
Subject specialisations: Quality fiction, new age, Scottish, nursing, foreign fiction and children's books.

MELVEN'S BOOKSHOP
29 Union Street, Inverness IV1 1QA
Tel: 0463 233500
Fax: 0463 711474
Contact: Malcolm Herron (Manager)
Subject specialisations: Scottish, general and paperback fiction.

Kirkcaldy

THE BOOK HOUSE
21-25 Tolbooth Street, Kirkcaldy, Fife KY1 1RW
Tel: 0592 265378
Contact: Morag Gunn (Manager)
Subject specialisations: Computing, Scottish and local interest.

Perth

JAMES THIN
176 High Street, Perth PH1 5UN
Tel: 0738 35222
Contacts: Sheila Lindsay (Manager); Miss Marion McGregor (Events)

WATERSTONE'S BOOKSELLERS
St John's Centre, Perth PH1 5UX
Tel: 0738 30013
Fax: 0738 43478
Contact: Louise Cassells (Manager)
Subject specialisations: Scottish, fiction, biography and children's.

St Andrews

J & G INNES LTD
107 South Street, St Andrews, Fife KY16 9QW
Tel: 0334 72174
Contact: Mrs P M Innes (Manager)
Subject specialisations: Scottish and local interest, general and children's.

JOHN SMITH & SON (GLASGOW) LTD
127 Market Street, St Andrews, Fife KY16 9PE
Tel: 0334 75122
Contact: Ken MacKenzie (Manager)
Subject specialisations: Paperbacks, maps, Scottish and local publications
(computer link to Glasgow).

Stirling

DILLONS THE BOOKSTORE
20-24 Murray Place, Stirling FK8 2DD
Tel: 0786 451141
Contact: Annabel Gibbs (Manager)

JOHN SMITH & SON (GLASGOW) LTD
The MacRobert Centre, University of Stirling, Stirling FK9 4LF
Tel: 0786 473891
Contact: John Gray (Manager)
Subject specialisations: Academic textbooks, general, children's books
and stationery.

Stornoway

RODERICK SMITH LTD
52 Point Street, Stornoway, Isle of Lewis PA87 2XF
Tel: 0851 702082
Contact: Mrs Irene Matheson (Manager)
Subject specialisations: Local, Scottish, Gaelic and children's books.

Tarbert

ANN R THOMAS GALLERY
Harbour Street, Tarbert, Argyll PA29 6UD
Tel: 0880 820 390
Contact: Ann Thomas (Proprietor)
Subject specialisations: Nautical books and charts, Scottish interest, cookery, gardening and children's books.

Ullapool

THE CEILIDH PLACE
14 West Argyle Street, Ullapool, Ross and Cromarty IV26 2TY
Tel: 0854 612103
Fax: 0854 612886
Contact: John Charity (Bookshop Manager)
Subject specialisations: Extensive range including biography, feminist, fiction, poetry, political and Scottish.

Scottish Book Centre

The idea of a Scottish Book Centre in Edinburgh, to meet the needs of the growing publishing industry and the development of literary promotions in Scotland, was first put forward in 1988. It is perhaps the largest single initiative for books in Scotland for several decades and a major move to restore Edinburgh to its former position of eminence within the publishing scene. The premises at Fountainbridge Library had been used as storage for some 20 years and the task of renovation was enormous. Internal walls and staircases were built, plaster restored, wood panelling renewed, plumbing and wiring replaced and from the dusty space, bright new facilities were created. Offices for the Scottish Publishers Association, the Edinburgh Book Festival and Book Trust Scotland have been created, together with conference and display facilities, space for meetings and book launches, for training courses and press briefings. Registered as an assessment centre for vocational training and qualifications in publishing, the Book Centre hosts programmes of author events, with display facilities available to teachers, librarians and booksellers. The Copyright Licensing Agency has taken some space to use as a Scottish base for its work.

To set up the project took a great deal of money and many funding bodies and sponsors made it possible; a full list is on display in the Scottish Book Centre. To them we owe many thanks. Ideas and suggestions for the use of the Scottish Book Centre are welcomed and we hope that all sections of the book world in Scotland will continue to make full use of this resource.

The T C Farries Room, which seats around 40 people in rows or 20-25 around tables, is available for meetings, conferences, book launches, prize awards and exhibitions. Kitchen facilities and cloakroom are adjacent to the room. The room is available for hire at a moderate charge to outside organisations whilst SPA member publishers may have free use of the room for one day per year. For booking details please contact the SPA on 031 228 6866. The room was provided for the Scottish Book Centre by T C Farries & Co Ltd, the major Scottish-based supplier to libraries in Scotland, the UK and world-wide.

Edinburgh Book Festival

EDINBURGH BOOK FESTIVAL
Scottish Book Centre, 137 Dundee Street, Edinburgh EH11 1BG
Tel: 031 228 5444
Fax: 031 228 4333
Company established: 1982 (Edinburgh Book Fair Ltd)
Contacts: Shona Munro (Director); Valerie Bierman (Children's Fair Organiser); Michelle Stars (Administrator)
Date of next Book Festival: 14-30 August 1993

Over 62,000 people visited the fifth Edinburgh Book Festival during the 17-day event in 1991. Coinciding with the highly-acclaimed Edinburgh International Festival of the Arts, the biennial Book Festival has celebrated the arts of writing, literature and reading since 1983. It continues to attract readers and non-readers, encourage young readers and to heighten public awareness of books and writing.

Much of the success of the Book Festival is due to its location in Charlotte Square Gardens, in the heart of Edinburgh's magnificent Georgian city centre. The Festival comprises a major book display and selling area, a Children's Book Fair, and two theatres, all housed in a series of marquees. The spectacular Beck's Spiegeltent, a 1920s mirror tent from Amsterdam provides an outstanding location for the bar/cafe and all-day cabaret stage. The site is arranged in a double-courtyard design allowing visitors to sit, eat, drink, listen to musicians and even read in the garden surroundings.

One of the most popular and important features of the Edinburgh Book Festival is the extensive programme of talks, discussions, demonstrations and readings. The festival has established a considerable reputation for producing a high quality, entertaining programme involving writers and media personalities from around the world, both new and established. Writers who have appeared in the past include Maya Angelou, James Baldwin, Garrison Keillor, Doris Lessing, William McIlvanney, Brian Moore, Ben Okri, Michael Ondaajte, Sara Paretsky and Mary Wesley.

The Children's Fair organises special events for school-parties, workshops, family events, storytellings and author talks. Thousands of young people are brought face to face with their favourite writers who have included Roald Dahl, Rolf Harris, Shirley Hughes, Terry Jones, Joan Lingard, Michael Palin, Terry Pratchett and Michael Rosen. Through the Book Display and Exhibition areas, the Book Festival also offers publishers an opportunity to show and sell the best of their lists. In 1991, visitors to the Book Festival bought over £141,000 worth of books. The Book Festival will remain a biennial event for the foreseeable future. The organisation is planning a *Meet the Author* series outwith festival time and to extend the touring opportunities for authors and literary events around Scotland.

Book Trust Scotland

BOOK TRUST SCOTLAND
Scottish Book Centre, 137 Dundee Street, Edinburgh EH11 1BG
Tel: 031 229 3663
Fax: 031 228 4293
Contacts: Lindsey Fraser; Kathryn Ross; Christine Young

Book Trust Scotland is an independent, educational charity which promotes reading. Our aim is for every child to be a reading child, every adult a reading adult and every reader a lover of good books.

The function of Book Trust Scotland is to disseminate information about reading throughout the country, and to do this we use a range of agencies depending on the focus of the project. For example, the recent *Books for Babies* campaign relied heavily on health visitors and carers to pass on the message. By using non-traditional outlets, in addition to libraries, bookshops and schools, we aim to reach a much wider public.

Our well-used book information service answers requests from all over the country and some from overseas. We hold information on most writers working in Scotland and have an extensive library of press cuttings on Scottish literary themes and issues. We also have access to a wide range of bibliographies, literary magazines and other resource materials.

A significant proportion of our activities takes place in the field of children's literature. our reference library receives a copy of every book published for children within the previous 12 months and is used by teachers, librarians, students, press and media and other interested individuals. It is also the venue for our Meet the Author events. We regularly compose reading lists and offer small exhibitions of books on specific subject areas. Another resource which is much in demand is our collection of children's books by Scottish writers and illustrators (including some books now out of print).

We produce and sell poetry posters, children's book posters and a variety of publications including the popular *Off The Shelf: A Directory of Children's Books and Writers From Scotland* and *Twentieth Century Scottish Classics* compiled and annotated by Edwin Morgan. A *Guide To Twentieth Century Scottish Women Writers* is in preparation. Book Trust Scotland administers the annual Kathleen Fidler Award and also ran the Hugh MacDiarmid Centenary Award and Prize in 1992.

Publishers, authors and agents are invited to keep us as up-to-date as possible with their activities. Only by being kept informed can we achieve our objective - a sustained increase in the reading population of Scotland.

Scottish Arts Council

SCOTTISH ARTS COUNCIL
12 Manor Place, Edinburgh EH3 7DD
Tel: 031 226 6051
Fax: 031 225 9833
Date established: 1967 as Scottish Arts Council
Contacts: Seona Reid (Director); Graham Berry (Director of Finance &
Administration); Andrew Nairne (Art Director); John Murphy
(Combined Arts Director); Anna Stapleton (Drama and Dance Director);
Walter Cairns (Literature Director); Matthew Rooke (Music Director)
Office hours: Mon-Thurs 9.00a.m.-5.30p.m.; Fri 9.00a.m.-5.00p.m.

Objectives
To develop and improve knowledge, understanding and practice of the
arts and to increase their accessibility to the public throughout Scotland.
A recent policy statement identified the Council's main aim as being to
"create a climate in which arts of quality flourish and are enjoyed by a
wide range of people throughout Scotland".

Activities
The Council itself does not administer orchestras, theatres, arts centres
or festivals, but grant-aids others to do so. Its officers act as assessors on
boards of management of many of these organisations which range in
scale from local festivals, community arts groups, guilds and clubs, to
major institutions, such as orchestras, opera and ballet companies,
regional theatres and major arts centres. Many of these, for example, the
opera, ballet, orchestras and some drama companies, tour widely
throughout Scotland. In addition, the Council subsidises about 100 arts
associations and music clubs serving towns and villages across Scotland,
which each year promote over 500 professional performances. Many of
these events are co-ordinated by the Council for the clubs and associations.

The Council also operates schemes for awards, bursaries, fellowships
and travel and research grants to writers, artists, composers, dancers,
actors, playwrights, choreographers and film-makers. A Council of 20
meets six times a year to formulate and oversee the policies of the SAC.

It is advised by a number of specialist art form committees and panels which are made up of people from all over Scotland who have expert knowledge of the arts and related interests.

Information
SAC offers a general advisory service on most aspects of the arts and publishes a number of reports, guides and bulletins about its work and the arts in Scotland in general. A list of publications is available from the Communications Department.

Literary Magazines
Published with subsidy from the Scottish Arts Council. These magazines may be obtained direct from the publishers or from bookshops.

Books in Scotland
Christine/Conrad Wilson, 15 Gloucester Place, Edinburgh EH3 6EE
Tel: 031 225 5646

Cencrastus
Raymond Ross, Workshop Unit 1, Abbeymount Techbase, 2 Easter Road, Edinburgh EH8 8EJ Tel: 031 661 5687

Chapman
Joy Hendry, 4 Broughton Place, Edinburgh EH1 3RX
Tel: 031 557 2207

Edinburgh Review
Murdo MacDonald, EUP, 22 George Square, Edinburgh EH8 9LF
Tel: 031 650 4215

Gairfish
Richard Price, 34 Gillies Place, Broughty Ferry, Dundee

Gairm (Gaelic)
Derick Thomson, 29 Waterloo Street, Glasgow G2 6BZ
Tel: 041 221 1971

Lallans (Scots)
David Purves, 8 Strathalmond Road, Edinburgh EH4 8AD
Tel: 031 339 7929

Lines Review
Tessa Ransford, Macdonald Publishing, Edgefield Road, Loanhead, Midlothian
Tel: 031 440 0246

New Writing Scotland
David Hewitt, c/o Department of English, Aberdeen University, Taylor Building, King's College, Aberdeen AB9 2UB
Tel: 0224 40241

Northlight
Anne Thomson, 136 Byres Road, Glasgow G12 8TD
Tel: 041 339 6151

Scottish Book Collector
Jennie Renton, 48 Keir Street, Edinburgh EH3
Tel: 031 228 4837

Tocher
Alan Bruford, School of Scottish Studies, 27 George Square, Edinburgh EH8 9LD
Tel: 031 650 4160

Verse
Robert Crawford, Department of English Literature, St Andrews University, St Andrews, Fife
Tel: 0334 76161

West Coast Magazine
Margaret Fulton Cook, 8A Caledonia Street, Paisley PA3 2JF
Tel: 041 427 7846

Scottish Poetry Library

SCOTTISH POETRY LIBRARY
Tweeddale Court, 14 High Street, Edinburgh EH1 1TE
Tel: 031 557 2876
Association established: 1982
Contacts: Tessa Ransford (Director); Penny Duce (Librarian)
Services offered: Borrowing and reference library; research assistance and information.
Description of services: The Scottish Poetry Library (SPL) opened in February 1984 with the aim of making the poetry that has been written in Scotland in Gaelic, Scots and English, particularly that of the twentieth century, more visible and accessible to the general public throughout the country.

The resources and services provided include the following:
a) Older Scottish poetry and an interesting selection of twentieth-century poetry from all over the world are available in the library. The poetries of Europe and of the rest of the world are also well represented.
b) Borrowing is free, apart from a charge of £0.50 per item borrowed by post. Freepost return labels are provided.
c) The SPL has a reference collection of around 7,000 items and lending stock of around 5,000 volumes. Printed catalogues of the lending collection have been published in 1988 and 1991 (price £5.00 for the two including postage); another supplement will update this in due course
d) The SPL has pioneered a computerised index to poetry called INSPIRE: INternational and Scottish Poetry Information Resource. This allows people to search for poetry under their own terms, controlled by a comprehensive thesaurus of subjects. Poetry can therefore be introduced under any topic and across the curriculum. Twenty Scottish literary magazines published over the past 40 years are also being indexed.
e) Current editions of literary magazines are on sale in the Library and back numbers may be consulted.
f) Audio- and video-tapes for borrowing and consulting are also provided. The stock of these is steadily increasing.

g) The SPL Newsletter keeps the membership, currently over 700 individuals and organisations, in touch. The annual subscription is £10.00 for individuals and £15.00 for organisations.

The SPL is situated in Tweeddale Court, off the Royal Mile. The courtyard is an attractive venue for informal poetry readings during the Edinburgh International Festival and at other times. The SPL provides accommodation for overseas poets-in-residence for purposes of cultural exchange and dialogue.

However, the SPL's activities are not confined to Edinburgh. Extension branches have been opened at the following addresses, where books may be borrowed:

  Craigie College of Education, Ayr
  Dept of Adult and Continuing Education, Glasgow University
  Hillhead Library, Glasgow
  Paisley Central Library
  Dudhope Arts Centre, Dundee
  Longpark Resource Centre, Kilmarnock
  Shetland Library, Lerwick
  Stornoway Public Library
  The Ceilidh Place, Ullapool

A van takes materials and information out into the community throughout Scotland. Such visits are arranged on request, as are also visits by special groups to the Library.

The Library is open from 12 noon until 6p.m. every day, except Thursdays, when the hours are from 2p.m. to 8p.m. It is normally closed on Sundays.

SCOTTISH LIBRARY ASSOCIATION

Motherwell Business Centre, Coursington Rd, Motherwell ML1 1PW
Tel: 0698 252526
Fax: 0698 252057
Company established: 1908
Contact: Robert Craig BA, MA, ALA (Director)
Services offered: Promotion of libraries and librarianship
Description of services: See below.

What is the Association?
The Scottish Library Association was founded in 1908 as an independent association. In 1931 it entered into union with the Library Association in Scotland. The Library Association, the professional body for librarians and information specialists in the United Kingdom, was founded in 1877 and received a Royal charter in 1898. It is a registered charity.

From only 65 members in 1908, the Scottish Library Association now has over 2,300 covering all aspects of library and information work. The expansion mirrors the development of library and information services and their increasing importance in many aspects of Scottish life.

What does it do?
The Association's main aims are the promotion of libraries and librarianship, the improvement of library services and the qualifications and status of librarians.
It pursues these aims by:
1. Producing and promoting standards for library and information services.
2. Presenting the views of members to central and local government, to COSLA, Royal Commissions, Committees of Inquiry and other bodies on a wide range of topics.
3. Negotiating and consulting with other national bodies involved in the cultural and educational life of Scotland.
4. Organising a wide range of meetings, conferences and weekend schools to keep members informed of developments in librarianship.

5. Advising members on careers, offering guidance on salary levels and co-operating with trade unions to improve salaries and conditions of service.

The Association ensures that the voice of the profession is heard on matters of major significance which affect library services.

Publications
The Association publishes a wide range of material including an annual survey of public library expenditure, a directory of Library and Information Resources in Scotland, and, with Magna Print Ltd, a large print series devoted to Scottish writers. It issues six times a year a magazine, *Scottish Libraries,* to enable members to keep abreast of new developments in the profession. The Association sponsors a biennial competition for the best publication produced by a library service.

How is it funded?
The Library Association derives its funding from members' subscriptions and by income generated from the sale of publications, conferences and short courses.

The way ahead
a) Establishing a Scottish Library Council as recommended in the COSLA report on Public Library standards.
b) Improving the co-ordination of library and information services.
c) Strengthening the role of library services in the community.

Publishing Notes

The process of transforming a manuscript into a book, a publication of quality, requires organisational skills and creative ideas together with a sound grasp of finance and a flair for marketing; a combination of talent and experience which is not easily perfected. A first step for all publishers, however, is to give their books a professional image by ensuring that the basic publishing conventions are followed; it is essential to obtain an ISBN, a bar code and to make available Cataloguing in Publication Data; it is mandatory to acknowledge copyright and to deposit copies of the book in the Copyright Libraries.

I S B N

International Standard Book Numbering is the system of giving to each book an unique 10-digit code which identifies that title (or one particular edition of the title) from one specific publisher. ISBNs are issued by:

The Standard Book Numbering Agency,
12 Dyott Street,
London WC1A 1DF
Tel: 071 836 8911

Bar Code

This allows the book's details to be read by electronic means at the point of sale in a bookshop (or at the issue desk in a library). Most bookshops use a system called Electronic Point of Sale (EPOS) which records each transaction and helps to manage the stock orders. Bar codes may be obtained from:

Kings Town Photocodes,
Waltham House, Riverview Road,
Beverley HU17 8DY
Tel: 0482 867321
Fax: 0482 882712
Symbol Services Ltd,
The Baltic Centre, Great West Road,
Brentford, Middlesex TW8 9BU
Tel: 081 847 4121
Fax: 081 847 4125

Cataloguing in Publication Data
Information about the British Library Cataloguing-in-Publication programme is available from:
Whitakers Bibliographic Services,
12 Dyott Street,
London WC1A 1DF
Tel: 071 836 8911
Fax: 071 836 2909

Copyright Libraries
Publishers in the United Kingdom and Ireland have a legal obligation to send one copy of each of their publications to the Legal Deposit Office of the British Library within one month of publication. Publications should be sent to:
Legal Deposit Office,
The British Library,
Boston Spa, Wetherby, West Yorkshire LS23 7BY
Tel: 0937 546267

Further copies must also be sent to the Bodleian Library Oxford; University Library, Cambridge; the National Library of Scotland; the Library of Trinity College, Dublin; and the National Library of Wales. These can be supplied by sending five copies for redirection to:
Mr A T Smail,
Agent for Copyright Libraries,
100 Euston Street,
London NW1 2HQ

Copyright
This is a complex and occasionally very technical area; there are books which explain the law more fully as it pertains to copyright in the UK and abroad (see Bibliography). Copyright only exists in material which can be defined as literary, dramatic, musical or artistic 'works', or any of the following 'subject matters': sound recordings, cinematograph films, television and sound broadcasts, cable programmes and published editions of works.

If a work is published in the UK during the author's lifetime, copyright subsists in the work until 50 years from the end of the year of the author's death. If a work is not published during the author's lifetime then copyright subsists until 50 years from the end of the calendar year in which it was first published. If a work is never published it remains in copyright. The Copyright, Designs and Patents Act 1988 has attempted to deal with the problem of ownership and copyright with regards to modern technology and associated new forms of storing, 'publishing' and retrieval of material. The moral rights of the author - the 'integrity' of the copyright holder - are also acknowledged by the Act. Further information may be obtained from:

The British Copyright Council,
29-33 Berners Street,
London W1P 4AA
Tel: 071 359 1895

Permissions for photocopying in academic and educational institutions are dealt with by:
Copyright Licensing Agency,
90 Tottenham Court Road,
London W1P 4AA
Tel: 071 436 5931
Fax: 071 436 3896

Copyright Permissions
It is normally the author's responsibility to obtain (and pay for) permission to quote written material which is still in copyright. Permission should always be sought from the publisher of the quoted work, not the author. In complex cases, such as an anthology, however, the publisher often does this work for the author. Fees for quotation vary : there is no standard scale. British copyright law allows free use of copyright material in certain circumstances. It is permissible to quote up to about 200 words for the purpose of review (where the extract is not 'substantial') but this does not apply to anthologies or poetry.

Acknowledgements

The sources of all in-copyright quotations (words or music), tables and illustrations should be given, whether or not it was necessary to obtain permission for their use. In law 'sufficient acknowledgement' means at least the author (composer, artist and so on) and title.

The Net Book Agreement

The Net Book Agreement (NBA) has been in existence in one form or another in Britain since 1900. It is in fact a publishers' agreement, under which rules are set out for the supply and sales of books through bookshops and other retailers. The current agreement has lasted since 1957, after its passage through the Restrictive Practices Court the previous year; it has recently been reviewed and was found still to be in the public interest.

Under the terms of the agreement, publishers are free to decide if they wish to publish their books at net prices or not. Once they decide to do so, the price cannot be reduced by a bookseller - nor indeed can it be raised.

The arguments for and against the Net Book Agreement have been raging in the press over recent years, but a majority of publishing companies and booksellers continue to support it. It is feared that to abolish the agreement would lead to such price wars, mainly around mass-market bestseller titles, that small businesses would be forced to close leaving fewer stockholding bookshops, less variety in choice of books, higher prices and fewer new titles. It is also feared that academic and scholarly books would be more expensive, and the possibility is noted that all books could carry higher recommended prices in order to allow discounting to look effective.

Grants to Publishers

SCOTTISH ARTS COUNCIL

The Literature Department, 12 Manor Place, Edinburgh EH3 7DD
Tel: 031 226 6051
Fax: 031 225 9833

In recognition of the pivotal position of publishing, extensive support is given to publishers in the form of grants towards the production costs of certain categories of books. The conditions and criteria attached to the 'Grants to Publishers' scheme and application form are available on request. Submissions from publishers are considered four times a year by a special panel, which then makes recommendations to the Literature Committee.

The Council also recognises the importance of a vigorous publishing industry in Scotland by making an annual grant to the Scottish Publishers Association to promote co-operative ventures such as exhibitions, joint mailings, representation at book fairs at home and abroad and so on. As Gaelic publishing is a specialist matter the Council gives an annual grant to the Gaelic Books Council which then assists the writing, production, promotion and selling of books worthy of support. The Association for Scottish Literary Studies is also supported by the Scottish Arts Council.

Prizes and Awards

JAMES TAIT BLACK MEMORIAL PRIZES
University of Edinburgh, Department of English Literature, David Hume Tower, George Square, Edinburgh EH8 9JX
Tel: 031 650 3619
Final entry date: 30 November
Presentation date: February
Value: £1,500 each
Frequency: Annual competitive
Description: One prize for fiction and one for biography, or work of that nature, first published in Britain in the previous 12 months. Supplemented by the Scottish Arts Council since 1979.

KATHLEEN FIDLER AWARD, THE
c/o Book Trust Scotland, Scottish Book Centre, 137 Dundee Street, Edinburgh EH11 1BG
Tel: 031 229 3663
Fax: 031 228 4293
Final entry date: 31 October
Presentation date: On publication
Value: £1,000 and guaranteed publication
Frequency: Annual competitive
Description: For a novel of 20,000-25,000 words for children aged 8-12. Authors should not previously have had a novel published for this age group. The award, suggested by Mary Baxter and Valerie Bierman, is sponsored by Blackie Children's Books and administered by Book Trust Scotland. The winning entry will be published by Blackie Children's Books.

HAWTHORNDEN PRIZE, THE
Hawthornden Castle, Lasswade, Midlothian EH18 1EG
Tel: 031 440 2180 or information regarding the prize from:
Lord Quinton, Chairman, Hawthornden Prize Committee, 42a Hay's Mews, Berkeley Square, London W1X 7RU
The Hawthornden Prize, the oldest of the famous British literary prizes, was founded in 1919 by Miss Alice Warrender. It is awarded annually

to a writer in English for the best work of imaginative literature. It is especially designed to encourage young authors and the word "imaginative" is given a broad interpretation. Biographies are not necessarily excluded. Books do not have to be submitted for the prize. It is awarded without competition. A panel of judges decides upon the winner.

MACALLAN/SCOTLAND ON SUNDAY SHORT STORY COMPETITION, THE

The Administrator, The Macallan/Scotland on Sunday Short Story Competition, 20 North Bridge, Edinburgh EH1 1YT
Tel: 031 243 3344
Final entry date: 26 February 1993
Presentation date: June 1993
Value: First prize: £5,000 and publication in Scotland on Sunday. Second prize: £250.
Frequency: Annual competitive
Description: Aimed at finding the best short story writer in Scotland. The maximum length for each short story is 3,000 words and up to three stories may be submitted. Stories must not have been previously submitted to this competition, published, performed or read on the radio. Entries are accepted from anyone born in Scotland, persons resident in Scotland and Scots living abroad.

AGNES MURE MacKENZIE AWARD, THE

The Saltire Society, 9 Fountain Close, 22 High Street, Edinburgh EH1 1TF
Tel: 031 556 1836
Fax: 031 557 1675
Final entry date: September 1993
Presentation date: End of 1993
Value: Amount varies
Frequency: Occasional, by nomination from professors of Scottish history.
Description: An occasional award for the most outstanding published work in the field of original research into Scottish history.

McVITIE'S PRIZE FOR THE SCOTTISH WRITER OF THE YEAR, THE

Deborah Watson, Michael Kelly Associates Ltd, Scottish Legal Building, 95 Bothwell Street, Glasgow G2 7HY

Tel: 041 204 2580
Fax: 041 204 0245
Final entry date: 31 August
Presentation date: November
Value: Scottish Writer of the Year: £10,000. Four other shortlisted writers: £500.
Frequency: Annual by nomination
Description: For the best substantial work of an imaginative nature published or performed between 1 September and 31 August. Novels, collections of short stories, poetry, biography, history and drama are all eligible. Writers must be born in Scotland, or be or have been resident in Scotland, or take Scotland as their inspiration.

PEOPLE'S PRIZE - FOR SCOTTISH FICTION

c/o John Linklater, Literary Editor, The Herald, 195 Albion Street, Glasgow G1 1QP or Robert Craig, Scottish Library Association, Motherwell Business Centre, Coursington Road, Motherwell ML1 1PW

Tel: 041 552 6255
Fax: 041 552 2288
Final entry date: Announced each year in *The Herald*
Presentation date: Announced each year in *The Herald*
Value: £5,000
Frequency: Annual
Description: A unique prize in that it is awarded by the vote of readers, not by the decision of panels of judges. Writers resident or born in Scotland are eligible for this prize which is sponsored by *The Herald* and administered by the Scottish Library Association through the Scottish Library Service which acts as returning officer. Readers throughout Scotland are invited to decide the winner by ballot from a short leet of six books reflecting the best of Scottish fiction. Previous winners have been delighted by this accolade from punters rather than pundits.

SALTIRE SOCIETY SCOTTISH LITERARY AWARDS, THE

The Saltire Society, 9 Fountain Close, 22 High Street, Edinburgh EH1 1TF

Tel: 031 556 1836

Fax: 031 557 1675

Final entry date: End of September

Presentation date: January

Value: Scottish Book of the Year: £5,000. Scottish First Book of the Year by a New Author: £1,500.

Frequency: Annual by nomination

Description: For a book on or about Scotland, or for a book with Scottish connections, not necessarily written by a Scot. Awards sponsored by *The Scotsman* and Scottish Television. Nominations made by literary editors.

SCOTTISH ARTS COUNCIL BOOK AWARDS, THE

Literature Department, Scottish Arts Council, 12 Manor Place, Edinburgh EH3 7DD

Tel: 031 226 6051

Fax: 031 225 9833

Value: £1,000 each

Frequency: Bi-annual (spring and autumn)

Description: A number of awards are given to new and established authors of published books in recognition of high standards of writing. Authors should be Scottish, resident in Scotland or have published books of Scottish interest. Entries from publishers only.

SCOTTISH INTERNATIONAL OPEN POETRY COMPETITION

c/o AWAS, School House, 108 Overtoun Road, Springside, Irvine, Ayrshire KA11 3BW

Tel: 0294 212382

Final entry date: 31 December

Presentation date: March

Value: £100 and MacDiarmid Trophy (UK section); International Trophy (International section); the Clement Wilson Trophy (Scots section). Diplomas are awarded to runners-up.

Frequency: Annual competitive

Description: The competition was inaugurated in 1972 and is the longest running of its kind in UK. Entry is free and submissions, limited to two per person, are acceptable from 1 September to 31 December each year. An SAE/International Reply Coupon must accompany entries.

SLOAN PRIZE, UNIVERSITY OF ST ANDREWS

Clerk of the Senate, The University of St Andrews, Fife KY16 9AJ

Tel: 0334 76161

Final entry date: 1 January

Presentation date: February

Value: £750

Frequency: Annual competitive

Description: The largest prize available for new writing in Scots. Donated by the London Burns Club in 1922, the prize is awarded for the best essay, short story, poem (up to a maximum of five per entrant) or play in Scots. No length is prescribed and only one entry per competitor will be considered. There is no entry fee or entry form. Submissions should be typed.

Book Design

MARK BLACKADDER
39 Warrender Park Terrace, Edinburgh EH9 1EB
Tel: 031 228 4237
Fax: 031 228 4237
Qualifications and experience: BA in graphic design. Fourteen years experience both in-house and freelance.
Services offered: Design, visualisation and finished artwork for books, magazines, journals and promotional material.
Description of services: Full design service from initial brief, visual and design to finished artwork. Clients include: The Amaising Publishing House Ltd, W Green, The Scottish Law Publisher, HMSO, Knox Press, Mercat Press, Saint Andrew Press, Scottish Book Marketing Group, Scottish Publishers Association.

DOUGLAS DOUGAN
3 Lower Joppa, Portobello, Edinburgh EH15 2ER
Tel & Fax: 031 669 0046
Qualifications and experience: Seven years' experience in-house and freelance.
Services offered: Comprehensive design package for books, magazines, journals and other printed material.
Description of services: Award winning design package: quality at a sensible price. Everything from initial brief to design and finished artwork. Fully computerised. Clients include: Whigmaleerie, Scottish Print Employers Federation, Scottish Dental Practice Board, BT and many other corporate and commercial publishers.

FRANCES GILBERT
3/6 Coinyie House Close, High Street, Edinburgh EH1 1NL
Tel: 031 556 4886
Qualifications and experience: Diploma in graphic design.
Services offered: Creative design and illustration.
Description of services: Book and jacket design and layout, maps, freehand illustration and calligraphy; also PageMaker DTP software. Clients include: Canongate Press, Link Housing Association, Scottish Child and Family Alliance and Speedwell Books.

JAMES HUTCHESON
7a Albany Street, Edinburgh EH1 3UG
Tel: 031 557 6369
Fax: 031 556 8720
Qualifications and experience: DipAD (Hons) Leeds, 18 years' experience.
Services offered: Graphic design and illustration (also in-house AppleMac system).
Description of services: Range from concept/visuals to design/illustration and finished artwork for the book and music industry. Clients include: Mainstream, Weidenfeld & Nicolson, Canongate, Chambers, CBS and Island Records.

PAUL MINNS
Cairnholy Old Farmhouse, Carsluith, Newton Stewart, Wigtownshire DG8 7EA
Tel: 055724 249
Services offered: Book design.
Description of services: Varied work includes *Automobile Association Directory*, *The Private Eye Story* and *Postman Pat*. Twice included in NBL Best 50 Books.

ANN ROSS PATERSON
9 Craiglea Place, Edinburgh EH10 5QA
Tel: 031 447 3183
Fax: 031 447 3183
Qualifications and experience: DA (Edin), 20 years in publishing.
Services offered: Graphic design and illustration.
Description of services: Graphic design from complete package including illustration e.g. *A Bunch of Sweet Peas*, Canongate, or design and layout e.g. *An Eye on the Hebrides*, Canongate, to cover design only e.g. all Polygon Fiction and (with illustration) *Carmina Gadelica*, Floris Books.

SMITH & PAUL ASSOCIATES

Balgonie House, Acer Crescent, Paisley PA2 9LN
Tel: 041 884 2212
Fax: 041 884 7802
Company established: 1992
Qualifications and experience: Design diploma, City & Guilds, Apple Macintosh trained, 15 years in-house experience.
Services offered: Visuals, design and layout to finished artwork for books, catalogues, magazines and promotional material.
Description of services: Overall design from initial brief, to finished artwork, for one, two and full colour publications. Clients include: Blackie Academic and Professional, The Saltire Society, Whittles Publishing, Scottish Print, Hamilton Publishers, W & R Chambers, Renfrewshire Enterprise.

Distribution

PENNY BLACK DISTRIBUTION LTD
35 Turnhouse Road, Edinburgh EH12 0AE
Tel: 031 317 7601
Fax: 031 339 6615
Company established: 1989
Contact: Tom J Welch
Services offered: Worldwide mailing services.
Description of services: International postage savings on normal mail rates for books, brochures, mailshots etc. An alternative UK mail delivery system to major UK cities. Envelope fulfilment, response handling and other mailing house services.

JILL DICK trading as SCOTTISH CULTURAL PRESS
PO Box 106, Aberdeen AB9 8ZE
Tel: 0224 586933
Fax: 0224 596933
Qualifications and experience: Nine years publishing/marketing/distribution.
Services offered: Publishing consultancy, marketing, distribution.
Description of services: Aimed particularly at small publishers (e.g. museums, libraries), individuals and societies, this service offers immediate entry within a well-distributed catalogue, central order and subscription fulfilment, customer service, and accounting packages. Consultancy during production, pre-publication marketing and publicity also undertaken. Leaflet production and associated services also provided.

Also see **Clan Books**, Wholesalers.

Bibliography:
Woodham, Roger (1988) *The Publisher's Guide to Distribution*, Blueprint (Chapman & Hall)

Editorial

ROSEMARY ADDISON
6 Buckingham Terrace, Edinburgh EH4 3AB
Tel: 031 332 1946
Fax: 031 332 1946
Qualifications and experience: BA (OU), Diploma Printing &
Publishing (Napier). Practice since 1978.
Services offered: Editorial, proofreading, production.
Description of services: Editing, proofreading, print preparation,
production/project management. Apple Macintosh in use.

MAGGIE M BEVERIDGE
Woodside, Kippen, Stirling FK8 3EL
Tel: 0786 870759
Qualifications and experience: BSc (Hons) Botany, five years' editorial
experience in STM publishing.
Services offered: Copy-editing and proofreading.
Description of services: Copy-editing and proofreading, books and/or
journals, particularly science and medicine.

BLACK ACE EDITORIAL
Ellemford Farmhouse, Duns, Berwickshire TD11 3SG
Tel: 03617 370
Fax: 03617 287
Qualifications and experience: Full details and samples of work available
on request.
Services offered: All text-processing and book production services.
Description of services: Total book production service. All stages from
typescript to finished books. Text capture, OCR scanning, disk
conversion, editing, laser proofs, typesetting, design, production and
delivery.

KATE BLACKADDER
39 Warrender Park Terrace, Edinburgh EH9 1EB
Tel & Fax: 031 228 4237
Qualifications and experience: Diploma in book and periodical publishing. Almost 20 years full-time and freelance publishing experience, in all departments.
Services offered: MS assessment, copy-editing and proofreading.
Description of services: MS reading and assessment. Copy-editing and proofreading (except scientific and technical). Previous employers/clients include: Hutchinson, Paul Harris Publishing, MacLean Dubois and Lochar. Current clients include: Scottish Equitable and Saint Andrew Press.

CALLUM BRINES
17 Huntly Gardens, Glasgow G12 9AT
Tel: 041 334 4013
Qualifications and experience: MA, MPhil Publishing, freelance since 1987.
Services offered: Computer-integrated editorial services, DTP training and consultancy.
Description of services: Conventional editorial skills plus writing, editing and producing reference books using Quark XPress and PageMaker on Apple Macintosh computers; expertise includes database publishing, DTP training and consultancy. Clients include: HarperCollins (Gem guides and travel), Cassell (dictionaries/reference), Larousse (pocket reference), Market House Books, Geddes & Grosset.

THORBJORN CAMPBELL
Gleniffer Place, 3 Miller Road, Ayr KA7 2AX
Tel: 0292 262359
Fax: 0292 262359
Qualifications and experience: MA (Hons), MLitt.
Services offered: Copy-editing, proofreading, indexing.
Description of services: Literary/academic books copy-edited. Proofreading and all classes of indexing undertaken.

EDITORIAL SERVICES
9 Binghill Drive, Milltimber, Aberdeen AB1 0JE
Tel: 0224 735821
Fax: 0224 733397
Qualifications and experience: Chartered Town Planner (MRTPI), Diploma in Philosophy (Dip Phil).
Services offered: Copy-editing and proofreading.
Description of services: Copy-editing and proofreading. We can deal with most subjects but we offer special skills in town planning and related subjects including planning law. Also in philosophy and related subjects and language skills (French and Russian).

PENNY HAYWOOD PR AND EDITORIAL
Communications House, 3 Lower Joppa, Edinburgh EH15 2ER
Tel & Fax: 031 669 5190 (fax ext;42)
Company established: 1986
Contacts: Penny Haywood (Editorial); Jackie Kane (Production)
Qualifications and experience: MA, FAIE, NUJ member, MIPR; 20 years in editing, design and print production.
Services offered: Editing and print production.
Description of services: Edit and produce in-house and external newspapers and magazines. Have electronic publishing in-house (IBM-based) as well as special knowledge of finance and a UK national finance columnist on the staff. Also cover general topics, arts, community relations etc. Clients include: BT, TSB and Barclays Bank.

BILL HOUSTON
45 Bridge Street, Musselburgh EH21 6AA
Tel: 031 665 7825
Qualifications and experience: BSc, BSc (Hons), DipLib, MPhil, MBiol, CBiol, MInfSci. Originally with Elsevier (Amsterdam): 19 years' experience as a freelance sub-editor.
Services offered: Editorial.
Description of services: Scientific/medical/technical editing and sub-editing. Copy-editing, proofreading, book and journal indexing, medical translations and abstracting.

DUNCAN McARA
30 Craighall Crescent, Edinburgh EH6 4RZ
Tel: 031 552 1558
Qualifications and experience: Diploma in Publishing; General Commissioning Editor, John Murray (1976-88); Assistant Editor, Faber & Faber (1972-6).
Services offered: Editorial consultant on all aspects of trade publishing.
Description of services: Editing, rewriting, copy-editing, proof correction. Subjects include art, architecture, archaeology, biography, film, military subjects and travel.

ROBYN MARSACK
10 Roxburgh Street, Glasgow G12 9AP
Tel & Fax: 041 334 2355
Qualifications and experience: DPhil (EngLit); 10 years' editorial experience.
Services offered: Editorial, translation (French).
Description of services: Editing, copy-editing, proofreading. General fiction and non-fiction, academic (humanities). Translations from French (non-technical). Current clients include: Carcanet, Faber & Faber, Yale. Member of SFEP, Society of Authors.

DOROTHY MITCHELL SMITH
5 Saxe-Coburg Street, Edinburgh EH3 5BN and 44 Brentham Way, Ealing, London W5 1BE
Tel: 031 556 2928 (ans) and 081 997 4580 (ans)
Fax: 081 997 6985 (bureau)
Qualifications and experience: In-house and freelance since 1970; Dip Cert Ed; NVQ Assessor.
Services offered: Project management, copy-editing, picture research, proofreading, training, NVQ assessment.
Description of services: Total editorial package including editing on screen. IBM-compatible computer in use with WordPerfect 5.1 software. Subject areas include art, architecture, archaeology, education (primary/ middle school), travel, leisure and academic (principally arts, but some science). BHTC and SFEP tutor in copy-editing skills.

JANE K ROBINSON

The Town House, 24 Castlegate, Jedburgh, Roxburghshire TD8 6AR
Tel: 0835 62122 or 0835 862122
Qualifications and experience: Eight years' continuous employment in all aspects of printing, four years in-house editor specialising in horticulture.
Services offered: Editorial and typesetting.
Description of services: Special skills: editing, typesetting, indexing, project management, meeting deadlines, liaising with authors/illustrators/photographic libraries/designers and printers. Computer literate. All work professionally executed to a high standard.

RONNIE SCOTT

11 Belhaven Terrace, Glasgow G12 0TG
Tel: 041 334 9577
Fax: 041 334 9577
Radiopager: 0345 333 111 (Pager No 0051029)
Mobile phone: 0850 730550
Qualifications and experience: BA English, 14 years in media, NUJ and BAIE member.
Services offered: Full editorial and production services.
Description of services: Writing, re-writing, ghost-writing, editing, video script-writing, publicity, desk-top publishing (Apple Macintosh with Quark XPress), newspaper and newsletter editing and design.

Also see: **David A Langworth,** Illustrators; **Charles S Coventry,** Indexers; **Dorothy Walker,** Indexers.

Illustration

ROB HAIN
Michaelmas Cottage, Lilliesleaf, Melrose, Roxburghshire TD6 9HX
Tel: 083 57 349
Qualifications and experience: BA (Hons) Fine Art, 13 years full-time professional.
Services offered: Paintings and drawings by commission.
Description of services: High quality children's picture-book illustration. Book jacket illustration children/adult. Bright, contrasted, idiosyncratic, full-colour acrylics on paper. Also b/w tonal pencil drawings in distinctive style. Please contact for examples.

DAVID A LANGWORTH
2 Dalkeith Street, Joppa, Edinburgh EH15 2HR
Tel: 031 669 6205
Qualifications and experience: Degree, Diploma in cartography, commercial publishing experience.
Services offered: Map design, editorial, drawing.
Description of services: Cartographic work: map design, editorial, final drawing of artwork for both black and white and colour maps. Text editing and proofreading.

CHRIS TYLER
8b Kildonan, Arnisort, Skye IV51 9PU
Tel: 047 082 346
Fax: 047 082 346
Description of services: Cartoonist and illustrator, fast fax service.

Indexing

A JANE ANGUS

Manse of Crathie, Brathie, Ballater, Aberdeenshire AB35 5UL
Tel: 033 97 42208
Qualifications and experience: BSc, FGS.
Services offered: Indexing.
Description of services: Indexes of geology, mineralogy, conservation and natural history, Scottish affairs and petroleum exploration texts: supplied on IBM-compatible disks if required.

CHARLES S COVENTRY

27/1 Jamaica Mews, Edinburgh EH3 6NL
Tel: 031 225 9414
Qualifications and experience: MA, BPhil, MLitt.
Services offered: Indexing, proofreading, translations (Gaelic), writing.
Description of services: Proofreading for arts subjects, languages, English, French, Latin, Greek (Classical), Gaelic. Indexing same fields and community newspapers, writing.

MARGARET CRONAN

47 Robb Place, Castle Douglas, Kirkcudbrightshire DG7 1LW
Tel: 0556 3265
Fax: 0556 3472
Qualifications and experience: BSC (Econ).
Services offered: Freelance indexing
Description of services: Prompt, reliable and accurate indexing services offered. Subject specialisms: economics, social sciences, political philosophy. Indexes supplied in IBM PC-compatible word processing disk form, if required.

BRITTON T J GOUDIE

6 Lime Grove, Scone, Perth PH2 6PE

Tel: 0738 51899

Qualifications and experience: LLM, registered indexer (Society of Indexers), over 20 years of indexing experience.

Services offered: Indexing.

Description of services: Specialising in: law (especially public international); international affairs; politics; history (ancient and 20th-century); biography.

CHANTAL HAMILL

128 Gowanbank, Livingston, West Lothian EH54 6EN

Tel: 0506 413554

Fax: 031 225 8329

Qualifications and experience: Indexes *Current Law Monthly Digest.*

Services offered: Indexing.

Description of services: Bilingual indexer (French/English), concentrating on 3 main subjects: the law; history and French studies.

ANNE McCARTHY

Bentfield, Gullane, East Lothian EH31 2AY

Tel: 0620 842247

Qualifications and experience: MA, ALA, registered indexer.

Services offered: Indexing.

Description of services: Indexes produced using full computer-indexing programme. Particular interest in medical sciences, Scottish and local history, sport, travel and guide books, biography and reference works.

DOROTHY WALKER

5 Calder House Rd, Mid Calder, Livingston, West Lothian EH53 0JZ

Tel: 0506 882462

Qualifications and experience: Qualified indexer and medical librarian.

Services offered: Indexing and proofreading.

Description of services: Index, proof-read material on medical/paramedical sciences; biography; countries and travel (Scotland); librarianship and information sciences; social sciences.

Industry-Related Organisations

ASSOCIATION OF AUTHORS' AGENTS

c/o 5th Floor, The Chambers, Chelsea Harbour, London SW10 0XF
Tel: 071 351 4763
Fax: 071 351 4809
Description of services: The AAA is a trade association of British agents. Members meet regularly to discuss matters of common interest and they observe a code of professional conduct. The Association liaises with other professional organisations nationally and internationally.

BOOK MARKETING LTD

7a Bedford Square, London WC1B 3RA
Tel: 071 580 7282
Fax: 071 580 7236
Contacts: Clare Middleton (Managing Director); Leslie Henry (Research Director)
Objectives: Provides information to help companies plan strategically and target marketing activity effectively and profitably.
Description of services: Development of the major ongoing syndicated survey *Books and the Consumer*; tailored private research for individual companies, both quantitative and qualitative; publications programme and information service; specialist activity, e.g. research, promotion, catalogue production; National Book Sale administration.

BOOKSELLERS ASSOCIATION: SCOTTISH BRANCH

Honorary Secretary, c/o James Thin, 53 South Bridge, Edinburgh EH1
Tel: 031 556 6743   **Fax:** 031 557 8149
Contacts: Nicholas Gray (Chairman); Patricia Britton (Honorary Secretary)
Objectives: The Association promotes and protects the interests of booksellers in the Scotland and the UK.
Description of services: Branch activities serve as a forum for the exchange of views between booksellers, and promote sales of Scottish books, Scottish authors, book token sales, booksellers clearing house and Scottish Book Marketing Group participation, maintaining close links with the Scottish Publishers Association.

BOOK TRUST SCOTLAND
Scottish Book Centre, 137 Dundee Street, Edinburgh EH11 1BG
Tel: 031 229 3663
Fax: 031 228 4293
Contacts: Lindsey Fraser (Executive Director); Kathryn Ross (Depute Executive Director); Chris Young (Secretary)
Services offered: Publications, information and advice.
Description of services: Promotion of reading. Book information and advice. General information about the book world. Specialities include children's and Scottish books. Reference library of current 12 months' children's books. Organisation of exhibitions, conferences and discussions.

BRITISH COUNCIL
Libraries, Books and Information Division
Medlock Street, Manchester M15 4PR
Tel: 061 957 7170
Fax: 061 957 7168
Contacts: Helen Meixner, Mary O'Neill
Objectives: To promote Britain and British ideas by helping to make British books available overseas, working closely with the UK book trade.
Description of services: 1. Provide high quality presence at a selection of international book fairs and exhibitions. 2. To publish guides to bookselling and market surveys in a number of countries helping to facilitate contacts between UK publishers and booksellers and possible overseas markets for their products.

CHRISTIAN BOOK PROMOTION TRUST
17 Rowan Walk, Crawley Down, West Sussex RH10 4JP
Tel: 0342 715889
Contact: Eric A Thorn
Services offered: See below.
Description of services: The Trust promotes donations of Christian books to public and school libraries.

FEDERATION OF CHILDREN'S BOOK GROUPS

c/o Sonas, Bank End Road, Bridge of Weir PA11 3EU
Tel: 0505 612472
Contacts: Mary Ann MacDonald, Thelma Simpson
Objectives: To bring children and their books together. We organise conferences nationally and regionally, run a unique and highly acclaimed Children's Book Award, hold National Tell-a-Story Week every year and have groups all over the country.
Description of Services: The Federation of Children's Book Groups is a voluntary, charitable organisation for parents and others who are interested in knowing more about children's books. Members are full of enthusiasm for children and their books and are prepared to do anything book-centred, anywhere!

GAELIC BOOKS COUNCIL, THE

Department of Celtic, University of Glasgow, Glasgow G12 8QQ
Tel: 041 330 5190
Contact: Ian MacDonald
Services offered: Publication and commission grants from the Scottish Arts Council; liaison between author and publisher; general information on all Gaelic books in print.
Description of services: Publishing of catalogues, typing of manuscripts, editorial work, including proofreading. The Council also retails Gaelic and Gaelic-related books and is willing to exhibit at special events. Welcomes invitations to visit libraries, bookshops and schools. Finances and occasionally organises literary events, such as poetry readings and talks on literary topics.

ILLUSTRATORS IN SCOTLAND
5 Cobden Crescent, Edinburgh EH9 2BG
Tel: 031 667 8592
Fax: 031 662 4631
Contact: David Sim
Description of services: Illustrators in Scotland was formed in December 1991 to promote the work of illustrators working in Scotland. A newsletter is produced and exhibitions organised. A contact list is kept of names and addresses of all illustrators involved in the Group.
The newsletter is produced three times a year. It contains articles and features on illustration and illustrators as well as information and addresses that may be of use to the group. The emphasis of the magazine is however on the illustrators' work and is very visual. Copies of the newsletter are sent free to design groups, advertising agencies and publishers. Contributions are invited from all working in the area.

INTERNATIONAL BOOK DEVELOPMENT LTD
10 Barley Mow Passage, London W4 4PH
Tel: 081 994 6477
Fax: 081 747 8715
Contacts: Tony Read, David Foster, Amanda Buchan, Carmelle Denning
Objectives: To work for the comprehensive development of book provision and book markets world-wide; to encourage investment in books and journals world-wide by governments, aid organisations and book trade bodies, backed by careful planning and implementation.
Description of services: 1. Provision of expert consultancy services world-wide to aid organisations, governments and book trade bodies. 2. Information and advisory services to publishers, booksellers and others on subscription. 3. Training services to aid-funded projects overseas. 4. Administration of the British Government's subsidised book schemes for developing countries (ELBS) and for central and eastern Europe (LPBB).

PIRA INTERNATIONAL
Scottish office: 1 Atholl Place, Edinburgh EH3 8HP
Tel: 031 228 2212
Fax: 031 228 1121
Contact: Michael Blackwood
Objectives: Pira International undertakes research, consultancy, educational activities and publishing (in the related areas of printing, paper and board and packaging industries).
Description of services: The Scottish office acts as a focal point for related industries in the north of England and Scotland. Consultancy work is carried out by the office in quality management, business planning and marketing. Technical assistance is sourced from the Leatherhead headquarters.

POETRY ASSOCIATION OF SCOTLAND
38 Dovecot Road, Edinburgh EH12 7LE
Tel: 031 334 5241
Contact: Robin Bell (Secretary)
Objectives: A registered charity, founded in 1924, promoting poetry in Scotland through readings and other events. All events are open to the public.
Description of services: We stage readings at the Netherbow Theatre, Edinburgh, and talks at the School of Scottish Studies, Edinburgh University. Our programme includes readings in the various languages of Scotland, plus many performances by poets from overseas. We also hold competitions and organise special events for schools and festivals.

SAPER (Scottish Association of Publishers' Educational Representatives)
c/o 23 Craighead Road, Bishopton, Renfrewshire PA7 5DT
Tel & Fax: 0505 862570
Contact: John Mitchell (Honorary Secretary)
Objectives: To give expression to opinion of members and to encourage a professional approach to the promotion of texts and materials in educational establishments throughout Scotland.
Description of services: SAPER provides a regular circular of information and requests for display materials to educational representatives of nearly all major publishers: items for inclusion can be sent to the Honorary Secretary (at the address above) from whom details of SAPER's regular diet of Scottish educational exhibitions are also available.

SCOTTISH LIBRARY ASSOCIATION
Motherwell Business Centre, Coursington Rd, Motherwell ML1 1PW
Tel: 0698 252526
Fax: 0698 252057
Contact: Robert Craig BA, MA, ALA (Director)
Services offered: Promotion of libraries and librarianship.
Description of services: See pages

SCOTTISH NEWSPAPER PUBLISHERS' ASSOCIATION
48 Palmerston Place, Edinburgh EH12 5DE
Tel: 031 220 4353
Fax: 031 220 4344
Contact: J B Raeburn (Director)
Services offered: Trade association for weekly newspaper industry.
Description of services: The Association is the employers' organisation/ trade association for the weekly newspaper industry in Scotland. The Association's main areas of involvement are industrial relations, education and training, advertising, newsprint, self regulation of the press and representations to government and others.

SCOTTISH PRINT EMPLOYERS FEDERATION

48 Palmerston Place, Edinburgh EH12 5DE
Tel: 031 220 4353   **Fax:** 031 220 4344
Contacts: J B Raeburn (Director)
Services offered: Trade association for the printing industry.
Description of services: The Federation is the employers' organisation/ trade association for all sectors of the printing industry in Scotland. The services offered to its 230 member companies are in the fields of industrial relations, education, training, commercial matters, representation to government, public bodies and others on matters directly affecting the industry. Member of Intergraf, the international confederation for employers' organisations in the printing industry.

SOCIETY OF AUTHORS, THE

84 Drayton Gardens, London SW10 9SB
Tel: 071 373 6642
Contacts: Mark Le Fanu (General Secretary); Alanna Knight, 24 March Hall Crescent, Edinburgh EH16 5HL (Scottish Secretary)
Services offered: Free booklet from London or Scottish Secretary.
Description of services: The Society is an independent union with 5,000 members. It offers advice on negotiations with publishers and broadcasting organisations, takes up complaints for members and pursues legal actions on their behalf. The Society provides members with a quarterly journal, *The Author*. As well as a London-based staff, the active Scottish branch, The Society of Authors in Scotland, holds regular meetings and takes up issues of concern to Scottish writers.

SOCIETY OF FREELANCE EDITORS & PROOF-READERS

c/o 16 Brenthouse Road, London E9 6QG
Tel: 081 986 4868
Contacts: Jane Sugarman (Secretary); Kathleen Lyle, 43 Brighton Terrace Road, Sheffield S10 Tel: 0742 685221 (Membership Secretary).
Services offered: The promotion of high editorial standards and recognition of members' professional status.
Description of services: Discussion meetings and talks, training courses and seminars, monthly newsletter (free to members).

SOCIETY OF INDEXERS, THE (Scottish Group)
Bentfield, Gullane, East Lothian EH31 2AY
Tel: 0620 842247
Contact: Anne McCarthy
Services offered: Contact point for everyone interested in the indexing of books, periodicals and other materials.
Description of services: The Scottish Group represents the society locally and aims to promote indexing amongst Scottish publishers and authors, to provide a contact for them and a forum for indexers. *Indexers Available in Scotland* is published and circulated regularly; it lists indexers and their specialised subjects.

STANDARD BOOK NUMBERING AGENCY
12 Dyott Street, London WC1A 1DF
Tel: 071 836 8911
Fax: 071 836 4343
Contact: Lars Andreasen (Manager)
Objectives: The Standard Book Numbering Agency Ltd is the National ISBN Agency for the UK and the Republic of Ireland.
Description of Services: The Agency issues new publishers joining the scheme with a publisher identifier. Where appropriate the Agency also creates, records and verifies individual ISBNs.

WOMEN IN PUBLISHING IN SCOTLAND
Contacts: June Nelson (membership), Tel: 031 343 6221; Rosy Addison (other information), Tel: 031 332 1946
Objectives: To promote the status of women working in publishing and related trades by providing them with the opportunity to meet and network. New members and offers of help are always welcome.
Description of services: WiPS was formed in 1991 from a group of women in publishing interested in meeting to discuss all issues concerning women working within the book industry. Our programme includes speaker meetings on the first Thursday of the month at The Filmhouse, Edinburgh, a regular newsletter and occasional training days. Affiliated to Women in Publishing (members can be included in their directory), c/o 12 Dyott Street, London WC1A 1DF.

96

Journalists and Writers

DAVID ALBURY
1 Shaw's Square, Edinburgh EH1 3NS
Tel: 031 556 4595
Qualifications and experience: Co-writer of *The Scottish Hotel Guide*.
Articles and crosswords in various publications, including *Computing*,
Big Farm Weekly, *Care Weekly*, *Financial Adviser* and various tourist
guides.
Services offered: Articles, crosswords, reviews (books, restaurants).
Description of services: Wide range of interests including food, computers
and literature. Prepared to research and write on any topic.

HAMISH BROWN
21 Carlin Craig, Kinghorn, Fife KY3 9RX
Tel: 0592 890 422
Qualifications and experience: Professional author/photographer of 30
years' standing.
Services offered: Any writing or photographic services on Scottish
subjects.
Description of services: Large library, in colour/black and white, of
Scottish subjects, sites, topography. Also Ireland, Morocco, world
travel. Commissions undertaken. Writing and lecturing by arrangement.

STEUART CAMPBELL
4 Dovecot Loan, Edinburgh EH14 2LT
Tel: 031 443 3687
Qualifications and experience: BA (Open), DipArch (Birm).
Services offered: Science writer.
Description of services: Writes about science and its applications for the
average reader. Specialises in physics and its application via technology,
but also writes about astronomy and the environment. Investigative
reporting, using science to solve problems; books, articles and reviews.

RENNIE McOWAN
7 Williamfield Avenue, Stirling FK7 9AH
Tel: 0785 61316
Qualifications and experience: 35 years in journalism, broadcasting and PR.
Services offered: Articles, scripts, books author.
Description of services: Writer/broadcaster on mountaineering, environmental subjects, Scottish history and literature, religious subjects, tourism and children's books.

RODDY MARTINE
5 Haddington Place, Edinburgh EH7 4AE
Tel: 031 557 3329
Fax: 031 557 3803
Qualifications and experience: Former editor *Scottish Field*, current editor, *Scottish Hotels* magazine.
Services offered: Freelance editor, author, journalist.
Description of services: Wide range of expertise on Scottish topics. Author of seven books on Scottish subjects. Editorial experience, over 20 years, of five Scottish periodicals. Contributor to complete range of newspapers at home and overseas.

KENNY MATHIESON
4 Rosebank Grove, Edinburgh EH5 3QN
Tel: 031 552 2560
Fax: 031 552 7271
Services offered: Freelance writer.
Description of services: Freelance writer, specialising in music (jazz, classical, folk); literature; general arts. Journalism, reference books, copy-writing; other subjects negotiable.

Library Suppliers

ALBANY BOOK COMPANY
30 Clydeholm Road, Glasgow G14 0BJ
Tel: 041 954 2271
Fax: 041 958 1198
Services offered: Public and school library supplier. (For further details see display ad on following page.)

JMLS LTD
24 Gamble Street, Nottingham NG7 4PJ
Tel: 0602 708021
Fax: 0602 787718
Contact name: Lance T Weatherall (Sales)
Services offered: Comprehensive acquisition service.
Description of services: Comprehensive monograph and continuation acquisition services provided to public libraries and schools. Full bibliographic and computer services; including subject bibliographies to individual specification, on-line ordering and research via "Libtel 2".

T C FARRIES
Irongray Road, Lochside, Dumfries DG2 0LH
Tel: 0387 720755
Fax: 0387 721105
Company established: 1982
Contacts: Peter Landale (Managing Director); Mary Nettlefold (Marketing and Sales Director)
Services offered: Supply of books and audio-visual materials to libraries, other organisations and individuals in the UK and throughout the world.
Description of services: T C Farries provides a quality service to meet the individual needs of its customers. The company has extensive stockrooms in Dumfries and in Hinckley, Leicestershire, from where librarians may make selections; a bibliographic service helps manage stock selection and acquisition and external databases are used to research incomplete obscure titles. Approval services are prepared weekly and lists are mailed to customers free.

ABc

Albany

Book

Company

| The Premier public and school library supplier in Scotland offers to assist publishers of Scottish Books. | Full worldwide retail and wholesale distribution service now offered from our computerised warehouse. |

CONTACT US NOW FOR DETAILS.

30 Clydeholm Road, Glasgow G14 OBJ
Tel: 041 954 2271
Fax: 041 958 1198

Literary Agents and Publishing Consultants

HUGH ANDREW & CAROL LAWTON, SEOL

2FL, 13 Roseneath Street, Sciennes, Edinburgh EH9 1SH
Tel & Fax: 031 228 6189
Services offered: Sales and marketing.
Description of services: Two-person team covering the whole of Scotland, representing much of the independent Scottish publishing industry with a variety of lists, concentrating on Scottish and children's.

DAVID FLETCHER ASSOCIATES

58 John Street, Penicuik, Midlothian EH26 8NE
Tel: 0968 673409
Fax: 0968 675723
Contacts: David Fletcher (Sales); Riet Cannell (Production); Deirdre Lothian (Editorial)
Qualifications and experience: David Fletcher has been involved in academic, general and professional publishing for over 30 years.
Services offered: 1. Advice on all publishing matters. 2. The preparation and production of books and journals.
Description of services: The firm offers two unique, high-quality services: 1. Advice on all publishing matters, from product origination to policy, production, promotion and marketing. 2. The preparation and production of books and journals mainly for academic, learned and professional bodies lacking publishing facilities of their own.

PAUL HARRIS

Whittingehame House, Whittingehame, Haddington EH41 4QA
Tel: 03685 369 (Office); 0386 619370 (Cellphone)
Fax: 03685 377
Qualifications and experience: 24 years in publishing, 17 as a publisher; author of 26 books.
Services offered: Marketing, project management and book packaging.
Description of services: Consultant to publishers in the UK and abroad. UK office for Gorenjski Tisk (Slovenian bookprinters). Complete research, layout, production of projects from contracts to finished books. Books for business.

DUNCAN McARA

30 Craighall Crescent, Edinburgh EH6 4RZ
Tel: 031 552 1558
Qualifications and experience: Diploma in Publishing; General Commissioning Editor, John Murray (1976-88); Assistant Editor, Faber & Faber (1972-6).
Services offered: Literary agent.
Description of services: Thrillers and literary fiction; non-fiction: art, architecture, archaeology, biography, film, military, travel (home 10%, overseas by arrangement). Preliminary letter with sae essential. No reading fee.

NEGOTIATE LTD

34 Argyle Place, Edinburgh EH9 1JT
Tel: 031 228 8899
Fax: 031 228 8866
Contact: Gavin Kennedy (Managing Director)
Services offered: Contract negotiation and consultancy.
Description of services: Consultants and negotiating assignments in all aspects of publishing and commercial business, including author's contracts and disputes. Negotiation skills training workshops presented monthly in Glasgow (and at Heathrow and Manchester). Brochure from Negotiate at address shown.

Literary Editors in Scotland

Scottish Dailies

Aberdeen - Evening Express
Contact: Raymond Anderson, PO Box 43 Lang Stracht, Aberdeen AB9

Aberdeen - Press and Journal
Contact: Norman Harper, PO Box 43 Lang Stracht, Aberdeen AB9 8AF

Dundee - Courier and Advertiser
Contact: Shona Lorimer, 7 Bank Street, Dundee DD1 9HU

Dundee - Evening Telegraph
Contact: Tom Malecki, 7 Bank Street, Dundee DD1 9HU

Edinburgh - Evening News
Contact: Hamish Coghill, 20 North Bridge, Edinburgh EH1 1YT

Edinburgh - The Scotsman
Contact: Catherine Lockerbie, 20 North Bridge, Edinburgh EH1 1YT

Glasgow - Daily Record
Contact: Russell Steele, Anderston Quay, Glasgow G3 8DA

Glasgow - Evening Times
Contact: Russell Leadbetter, 195 Albion Street, Glasgow G1 1QP

Glasgow - The Herald
Contact: John Linklater,195 Albion Street, Glasgow G1 1QP

Greenock Telegraph
Contact: Stewart Peterson, 2 Crawfurd Street, Greenock PA1 1YA

Paisley Daily Express
Contact: Anne Dalrymple, 14 New Street, Paisley PA1 1YA

Scottish Sunday Papers

Dundee - The Sunday Post
Contact: David Burness, Albert Square, Dundee DD1 9QJ

Edinburgh - Scotland on Sunday
Contact: Alan Taylor, 20 North Bridge, Edinburgh EH1 1YT

Photographers

HAMISH BROWN SCOTTISH PHOTOGRAPHIC

21 Carlin Craig, Kinghorn, Fife KY3 9RX
Tel: 0592 890422
Fax: 0592 640291
Services offered: Writing and photographic.
Description of services: Specialist writer/photographer specialising in Scottish, travel, outdoor activities etc. Large colour/b&w library. Has contributed to over 100 publications worldwide; edited anthologies, drawn maps, provided cover material. Regular lecturer.

STEPHEN J WHITEHORNE

164 Great Junction Street, Leith, Edinburgh EH6 5LJ
Tel: 031 555 4005
Qualifications and experience: Dip AD photographic studies and eight years as a professional photographer.
Services offered: Commissioned photography and picture sales.
Description of services: Commissioned photography and picture sales from stock transparencies. Subjects include Scottish landscape, travel, environmental, English landscape, general editorial, press and portraiture. Clients include: Scottish Tourist Board, Cassell Publishers, John Donald publishers, Forestry Commission, Channel 4, Shaw Design. Very competitive rates.

ALLAN WRIGHT PHOTOGRAPHY

The Stables, Parton, Castle Douglas, Dumfries and Galloway DG5 3NB
Tel: 06447 260
Fax: 06447 202
Services offered: Publishing, photography, photo library.
Book imprint: The Cauldron Press Ltd.
Description of services: Publisher of cards, prints, calendars. Book publisher of own material - The Cauldron Press Ltd. Photographer - commissions considered. Photo library includes S W Scotland, N Sea Oil, general landscape and nature.

Photographic Libraries

EDINBURGH PHOTOGRAPHIC LIBRARY
54 Great King Street, Edinburgh EH3 6QY
Tel: 031 557 3405   Fax: 031 557 1187
Company established: 1986
Contacts: Helen Henderson; Kate Johnston
Services offered: Loan of transparencies for purposes of reproduction.
Description of services: The Edinburgh Photographic Library holds a large selection of colour transparencies in all formats of Scottish subjects including industry, buildings, landscape, social and leisure activities, wildlife and matters of historic interest. Archival material also available.

DAVID WILLIAMS PICTURE LIBRARY
50 Burlington Avenue, Glasgow G12 0LH
Tel: 041 339 7823   Fax: 041 337 3031
Qualifications and experience: Seven years' experience of writing travel books. Four years' experience of running a picture library. Member of the British Association of Picture Libraries and Agencies.
Services offered: Supply of colour transparencies for reproduction.
Description of services: Supply of medium format and 35mm colour transparencies of Scotland and Iceland. Subjects include towns, villages, landscapes, historical buildings etc. Commissions undertaken. Catalogue available. Travel books and articles written.

STILL MOVING PICTURE COMPANY
67a Logie Green Road, Edinburgh EH7 4HF
Tel: 031 557 9697   Fax: 031 557 9699
Company established: 1991
Contacts: John Hutchinson; Sue Hall
Services offered: Stock photography (still and moving).
Description of services: Over 200,000 pictures of Scotland - the country, its people and its business - other countries worldwide and over 24 hours of movie film, hence still and *moving*, Scotland's largest stock photo and film library with worldwide coverage.

Also see: **Colin Baxter Photography**, SPA member publishers; **Hamish Brown**, Photographers; **Alan Wright Photography**, Photographers.

Print Production Consultant

ERIC MITCHELL
304 Kirkintilloch Road, Bishopbriggs, Glasgow G64 2HF
Tel: 041 772 1306
Fax: 041 772 1306
Services offered: Book production and print buying.
Qualifications and experience: Book production director (25+ years).
Description of services: Advice on all aspects of book production from specification of format, paper and manufacturing processes to detailed analysis of quotations; co-ordination of production from copy to delivery of finished product; liaison between publisher and supplier.

Hunter & Foulis Limited
Bookbinders

THE INDEPENDENT UK TRADE BOOKBINDER
FOR ALL YOUR BINDING NEEDS.

CASED BINDING   –   Max size 370mm x 310mm x 76mm
                      Min size 105   x 73   x 2mm

───────── *"THIN BOOKS A SPECIALITY!"* ─────────

LIMP BINDING   –   Max size 430mm x 280mm x 38mm
                      Min size 100   x 80   x 2mm

WIRE-O BINDING   –   Books – Max wire edge 445mm
                      Calendars – Max wire edge 614mm
                      Wire diameters from 5-25mm

───── *"THE COMPLETE RANGE OF WIRE-O STYLES AVAILABLE!"* ─────

FINE BINDING   –   Limited Editions, De Luxe Leather
                      Binding, Presentation Folders.

LOOSE LEAF   –   High quality loose leaf binders covered
BINDERS   in cloth or leather.

**FOR QUICK, PROFESSIONAL SERVICE –
PHONE US ON 031 556 7947, OR FAX 031 557 3911.
HUNTER & FOULIS LTD, McDONALD ROAD, EDINBURGH EH7 4NP**

QUALITY: TAKEN AS READ!

BPCC-AUP Ltd are proud to offer the all Scottish service for the Scottish publisher.

PRODUCTS

- Directories
- Catalogues
- Books
- Journals
- Magazines
- Yearbooks
- Looseleaf

SERVICES

- Typesetting
- DTP Bureau Service
- Web & Sheet-fed Printing
- Cased & Limp Binding
- Looseleaf Production
- Mailing & Distribution

Please call Joe Miller on 041 774 3377 to find out how our service will meet your needs.

BPCC-AUP Ltd
72 Coltness Street, Queenslie Industrial Estate, Glasgow G33 4JD
Tel. 041 774 3377 Fax. 041 774 0435

Printing and PoS Manufacture

BPCC-AUP Aberdeen Ltd
Hareness Road, Altens Industrial Estate, Aberdeen AB1 4LE
Tel: 0224 249639
Fax: 0224 249699
Contacts: Murray Webster (Sales)
Services offered: Sheet fed printing, limp binding, mailing.
Description of services: We are specialists in the production of books, journals and loose-leaf products. Working closely with BPCC-AUP Glasgow on the typesetting side, we are proud to offer the complete production service for the Scottish publisher.

HUNTER & FOULIS LTD
Bridgeside Works, McDonald Road, Edinburgh EH7 4NP
Tel: 031 556 7947
Fax: 031 557 3911
Company established: 1857
Contacts: Harry Waugh (Sales); Ken Mowbray (Sales); Barry Ashworth (Production)
Services offered: Bookbinding.
Description of services: We bind all types of publishers' books - cased/hard covers; paperback; wire-o; fine leather deluxe editions, presentations copies - from sheets printed all over Scotland and UK as a whole. Personal service. Company has considerable experience and capacity.

CLARK STEPHEN
447 Alexandra Parade, Glasgow G31 3AB
Tel: 041 554 8801
Fax: 041 554 7911
Company established: 1935
Contact: Gwen McCowan
Services offered: Point of sale, screen print, packaging.
Description of services: Manufacturers of point of sale material: dumpbins, 3D displays, counter packs, dummy books, packaging, posters, stickers and rigid slipcases.

MCQUEEN — PRINT DIVISION

McQueen Print are specialists in printing *fast* turnaround, low volume single and multicolour limp-bound books.

We make books for publishers selling to the *software*, *academic*, *educational* and *religious* book markets.

We are registered under BS5750.

McQueen Limited
Langlee Industrial Estate
GALASHIELS
Scotland
TD1 2UH
Telephone 0896-4866
Fax 0896-58485

CROMWELL PRESS LTD
Broughton Gifford, Melksham, Wiltshire SN12 8PH
Tel: 0225 782585
Fax: 0225 782659
Company established: 1991
Contacts: John Turner, Mike Arkell (Sales); Allan Hicks (Production)
Services offered: Printing and binding, bookwork manufacture.
Description of services: We service publishers with the manufacture of books, journals and loose-leaf works. The latest pre-press technology is employed to achieve a cost effective product to short production schedules. In-house production from receipt of camera copy to delivery ensures the quality, service and communication controls necessary to fulfil our customers' needs.

ORCADIAN LTD, THE
PO Box 18, Victoria Street, Kirkwall, Orkney KW15 1DW
Tel: 0856 873249
Fax: 0856 873978
Company established: 1789
Contacts: James Miller (Sales); Stewart Davidson (Production)
Services offered: All commercial printing, books, newspapers.
Description of services: Modern typesetting and printing machines enable us to compete with others less geographically remote.

McQUEEN LTD
Langlee Industrial Estate, Galashiels TD1 2UH
Tel: 0896 4866
Fax: 0896 58485
Services offered: Bookprinting and binding.
Description of services: See display advert.

Further Education

CENTRE FOR PUBLISHING STUDIES, THE
University of Stirling, Stirling FK9 4LA
Tel: 0786 73171 **Fax:** 0786 51335
One-year postgraduate course in Publishing Studies, giving an overview of industry structure, varieties of jobs, kinds of editing, production (including word-processing, desktop publishing and computer-typesetting). Graduates have mainly found editorial and marketing jobs in Scotland and England; others are in production control, bookselling or related fields. Further information available from the above address.

DEPARTMENT OF PRINT MEDIA, PUBLISHING AND COMMUNICATION
Napier University, Colinton Road, Edinburgh EH10 5DT
Tel: 031 444 2266 ext 2564 **Fax:** 031 452 8532
Full-time, three-year BA degree in Publishing, building on strengths of Diploma in Publishing offered since 1968. Cognate courses include Journalism, Public Relations, Advertising and Printing Management. The Department also offers customised in-service courses for publishing houses and related organisations in a number of fields from copywriting to new production technology. The Department houses the Scottish Colour Centre. Further information available from the above address.

SCHOOL OF LIBRARIANSHIP AND INFORMATION STUDIES
Robert Gordon University, 352 King Street, Aberdeen AB9 2TQ
Tel: 0224 262000 **Fax:** 0224 639559
Applicants who wish to enter the traditional publishing/bookselling sectors, the areas of the industry producing serials, magazines or the newer electronic media, may enter the full-time, three-year BA course or the four-year BA (Hons) course. Areas of study include print technology, retailing, business studies, editorial studies, design, mass communication and information technology. Further information from the secretary at the above address.

NATIONAL VOCATONAL QUALIFICATIONS

NVQs have now been established across many sectors of British industry, including publishing, in which a range of occupational standards has been defined and offered to employers and employees.

The Scottish Book Centre is registered as a centre for National Vocational Qualifications and offers NVQ assessment in several occupational areas to staff working in the publishing industry in Scotland, both as full-time employees and as freelance workers.

Enquiries concerning NVQs to: Lorraine Fannin, SPA, Scottish Book Centre, 137 Dundee St, Edinburgh EH11 1BG

PUBLISHING QUALIFICATIONS BOARD

Book House, 45 East Hill, Wandsworth, London SW18 2QZ
Tel: 081 871 1989
Fax: 081 870 8985
Company established: 1991
Contact: Rosie Thom
Services offered: National Vocational Qualifications.
Description of services: Administer and award National Vocational Qualifications covering nine occupational areas in publishing.

SCOTTISH PUBLISHERS ASSOCIATION
Skills Development Programme

A comprehensive programme runs annually from March to November, covering vital topics including editing, publicity, copyright and contracts, print production, financial management and direct marketing. Courses are led by practitioners in each field and popular seminars provide the opportunity to meet informally with others in the book trade. The programme offers substantial savings on courses held outside Scotland. The courses are open to everyone, with SPA and SBMG members enjoying preferential rates. Contact the SPA for a course brochure.

Further training information is available from:
Book House Training Centre, 45 East Hill,
Wandsworth, London SW18 2QZ

Translation

INTERLANG
56 High Street, Kirkcudbright, DG6 4JX
Tel: 0557 30814
Fax: 0557 31538
Qualifications and experience: 20 years' literary and technical work.
Services offered: Literary translation from French and German.
Description of services: Sensitive and insightful translation into English language of contemporary French- and German-language novels, short stories, essays, etc. Scientific and technological documents, Patent specifications, etc, translated with highest reliability and accuracy. Prompt return times. Communications by post, fax or e-mail.

Typesetting

BPCC-AUP GLASGOW LTD

72 Coltness Street, Queenslie Industrial Estate, Glasgow G33 4JD
Tel: 041 774 3377
Fax: 041 774 0435
Contact: Joe Miller (Sales Manager - Scotland)
Services offered: Technical typesetting, DTP bureau services, loose-leaf service.
Description of services: We offer all typesetting services, specialising in highly complex typesetting, DTP bureau work, loose-leaf setting and diary setting. We are able to accept all forms of input (e.g. manuscript, disc, mag tape, modem link) and together with our printing plant in Aberdeen, pride ourselves in giving the complete service to the Scottish publisher.

COMBINED ARTS

16a Carlton Street, Edinburgh, Lothian EH4 1NJ
Tel & Fax: 031 332 6580
Company established: 1985
Contacts: William Howes (Sales); Thomas Fleming (Production)
Description of services: Books, magazines, journals and reports designed and set from disc or hard copy to the highest standards of typographic excellence, for clients large and small in publishing, business and local government; from Carcanet and EUP to Scottish Equitable, R.S.A., and Lothian Regional Council. Call us today for an informal discussion of *your* needs.

Also see **Jane K Robinson,** Editorial Services.

Wholesalers

BOOKSPEED
48 Hamilton Place, Edinburgh EH3 5AX
Tel: 031 225 4950
Fax: 031 220 6515
Company established: 1986
Contacts: Kingsley Dawson (Director); Annie Rhodes (Director)
Services offered: Wholesaling.
Description of services: Scotland's largest wholesaler - with 14,000 titles; four reps covering Scotland, next day service and new title subscription service.

CLAN BOOKS
The Cross, Doune, Perthshire FK16 6BE
Tel: 0786 841330
Fax: 0786 841326
Company established: 1969
Contacts: Jonathon Hildray (Sales); David Warburton (Production)
Services offered: Clan Books stock, promote and distribute any publication suitable for the Scottish retail market. Customer advisory sales and delivery facilities operate with a personal, telephone and postal service to all parts of the country, throughout the year.
Description of services: Stockholding of general and Scottish interest publications, and distribution to the retail trade throughout Scotland.

GARDNERS BOOKS
Eastwood Road, Bexhill-on-Sea, East Sussex TN39 3PT
Tel: 0424 224777
Fax: 0424 220560
Date established: 1986
Contact: Bob Jackson
Services offered: A comprehensive range of wholesaling services.
Description of services: Over 45,000 titles available from 300 publishers. All orders despatched the same day for next day delivery if received by 16.30p.m. Full sales representation, experienced customer care support, Gardlink electronic ordering and information system. Monthly new title catalogues and bar coded re-order slips.

LOMOND BOOKS

36 West Shore Road, Granton, Edinburgh EH5 1QD
Tel: 031 557 2261
Fax: 031 552 1703
Company established: 1981
Contacts: T A Maher; D Baxter
Description of services: We wholesale and distribute through van sales and carry out merchandising throughout all of Scotland.

Writers and Writing

WRITERS' GROUPS AND WHERE TO FIND THEM

Despite the increasing difficulty which most aspiring writers have in finding a publisher for their work, the number of writers' groups in Scotland is steadily growing. For more information on arts/writers groups contact your local/regional libraries and district council leisure and recreation department. Other helpful addresses are listed below.

Scottish Association of Writers, Strathkelvin Writers Group, 30 Cloan St, Bishopbriggs, Glasgow G64 2HL
Contact: Mrs Sheila Livingstone (President of Scottish Association of Writers) Tel: 041 772 5604 (also for **Strathkelvin Writers Group**)
Will provide a list of at least 20 affiliated writers groups throughout Scotland. Also for help with publicity and marketing, mailing lists and mustering interested audience.

Writers Groups

Aberdeen Writers, 20 Duthie Terrace, Aberdeen AB1 6LQ
Contact: Mrs Ann Nicol, Tel: 0224 317523

Ayr Writers Club, Seafield Road, Ayr KA7 4AA
Contact: Mr A B Scott, Tel: 0292 286467

Blank Page, 4 Clarence Drive, Glasgow G12
Contact: Mrs C Richard, Tel: 041 339 2910

Dumfries Writers Workshop, 12 Hillview Drive, Dumfries DG1 4DS
Contact: Peter Fortune, Tel: 0387 65555

Dumfries Writers Workshop, 6 Merkland Farm Road, Bankend, Glencaple, Dumfries DG1 4RN
Contact: Charles Anderson, Tel: 0387 77442

Dundee University Writers Group, 2 Grangehill Drive, Monifieth, Dundee DD5 4RH
Contact: Valerie Cuming, Tel: 0382 533254

Edinburgh Writers Club, 3 Craigcrook Road, Edinburgh EH4 3NQ
Contact: Margaret McArthur, Tel: 031 332 9808

Elgin Writers Group, 67 McIntosh Drive, Elgin, Moray IV30 3AW
Contact: Jane Craig, Tel: 0343 545326

Glasgow Writers Club, 95 Great Western Road,Glasgow G4 9AH
Contact: Miss Sandra Adair

Greenock Writers Club,3 Lyle Place,Fort Matilda,Greenock,Inverclyde
PA16 7QS
Contact: Miss Lesley B Crawford,Tel: 0475 1234

Kinlochbervie Writers Group, Rhivichie Rhiconich, Lairg,Ullapool
IV27 4RA
Contact: Carol Forbes, Tel: 0971 521230

Kirkcaldy Women Writers,18 Mid St, Parkhead Gdn Village, Kirkcaldy
Contact: Mrs MacDougal, Tel: 0592 2615966
Other information: The group was started by the Workers Education
Association. It meets at the volunteer centre on a Friday.

Perthshire Writers Group, 75 Dunkeld Road, Perth PH1 5RP
Contact: Mrs Ada Ferguson

Scottish Association of Writers, Rowan Cottage, Station
Road,Garmouth, Elgin, Moray IV32 7LZ
Contact: Pat Bingham, Tel: 034387 267

Ullapool Writers Group, 2 Moss Road, Ullapool,Wester Ross
Contact: Phil Ellis,Tel: 0854 612151

Writers Workshop, 3 Hareshaw Bank, Tweedbank, Galashiels TD1
3RE
Contact: Tom Murray, Tel: 0896 55117

NOTES ON GETTING PUBLISHED

The manuscript/typescript

Manuscripts for presentation to a publisher should be easy to handle and read and complete in all details. The MS therefore should fulfil the following requirements:

1 It should be typed on one side of the paper, double-spaced throughout with good margins. The top copy should be sent to the publisher.

2 The pages should be numbered throughout. Late additions should be written on separate sheets and numbered, e.g, 10a.

3 If possible, use A4 paper.

4 It is not necessary for an author to give directions on his/her MS for type style.

5 Illustrations should be separate from the MS and each one numbered for identification, with captions and corresponding numbers typed together on a separate sheet.

Sending the typescript to a publisher

Your typescript is prepared, but now where do you send it? In *The Writers' and Artists' Yearbook* you will find a list of publishers and their addresses. There is also a brief description of the type of book each company publishes. It is intended to be a very rough guide so it is often better to browse in a good bookshop or library and see which companies produce the type of material you have just written. If you discover that a company has just produced a new work on your subject it is highly unlikely that it would favour another book in the same field so soon.

When you have selected a publisher, write first asking whether or not you may submit your work. Tell the publisher briefly what it is about. Give a few details about the market you intend it for, with some information on your qualifications for writing such a work. Be brief, and business-like. Send an sae with your enquiry. If the publisher is willing to consider the book, then post it to him enclosing postage for its return. Always retain a copy of your MS. A publisher might need to retain a MS for some time, so you may find you need your extra copy.

INTERNATIONAL PEN CENTRE
The Honorary Secretary, 33 Drumsheugh Gdns, Edinburgh EH3 7RN
Tel: 031 225 1038
Date established: Internationally, 1921; Scottish Centre, 1927
Contact: Laura Fiorentini, Honorary Secretary

PEN is a world association of writers. PEN stands for Poets/Playwrights, Editors/Essayists and Novelists, but membership is open to all published writers, including translators who subscribe to the aims set out in the PEN Charter. Briefly the charter calls for good understanding and mutual respect between nations and for freedom of expression everywhere.

PEN emerged as a writers' response to the Great War and it was founded in 1921 in the belief that writers, given freedom to transmit their thoughts within each nation and between nations, have much to contribute to international understanding and goodwill. The importance of PEN is that it is an international organisation linking writers from almost every country in the world. It is recognised by UNESCO as the voice of the international community of writers. There are over 100 centres throughout the world. It is one of the very few international organisations so far, in which Scotland is a full member in its own right.

Each centre runs its own domestic affairs, making its own rules within the framework of the international constitution and fixing its own programmes and subscriptions. But membership of any centre confers membership of all and the right to attend international meetings. The international office-bearers are elected, and the international activities are decided, by the delegates from national centres attending Assemblies of Delegates. Those activities include the assistance of writers who have been exiled or imprisoned for exercising their freedom of expression. Partly on the initiative of the Scottish Centre, PEN is now looking into the treatment of lesser-known languages (which, of course, include Gaelic and Scots). The international meetings, which are held each year in a different country, provide a unique opportunity for writers to meet, exchange views and get to know one another.

The Scottish Centre of PEN, established in 1927, owes its existence to the initiative of Hugh MacDiarmid. Over the years it has included in its membership most of the best known of Scottish writers, including Sir James Barrie, Neil Gunn, Eric Linklater and Sir Compton Mackenzie. There are at present about 170 members, including - besides eponymous categories of PEN - writers of critical, historical, scientific, travel, mountaineering and children's books, journalists and radio and television writers.

In 1934, 1950 and 1970, annual international meetings were held in Scotland. The centre hopes to be able to host another conference in the 1990s.

The centre has no premises of its own, but organises winter meetings in Edinburgh and Glasgow and a summer meeting elsewhere in Scotland. The annual programme includes literary talks and discussions, readings, informal parties for members and guests, and at least one reception, lunch or dinner in honour of a distinguished member or visiting writer. In recent years, Heinrich Boll, Chinhua Achebe, Nadine Gordimer, Brian Moore, Mario Vargas Llosa and Muriel Spark have been entertained.

Applications for membership are welcome from all published writers. A form can be obtained from the Honorary Secretary at the above address. The annual subscription (of which a large part goes towards the international activities of PEN, including support of imprisoned writers) is £15.00.

Bibliography

Book Production:
Barnard, Michael (1991) *Introduction to Printing Processes*, Blueprint (Chapman & Hall)
Peacock, John (1989) *Book Production*, Blueprint (Chapman & Hall)
Peacock, John, Berrill, Charlotte and Barnard, Michael (1992) *The Print and Production Manual*, Blueprint (Chapman & Hall) Williamson, Hugh (1983) *Methods of Book Design*, 3rd edn, Yale University Press
* *Book Production Practice* (1978), British Printing Industries Federation & The Publishers Association
The International Directory of Printers (1992), Blueprint (Chapman & Hall)
The Print Price Guides (1992), Blueprint (Chapman & Hall)
* *Scottish Print Directory* (annual) Scottish Print Employers Federation, 48 Palmerston Place EH12 5DE

Book Trade Information:
* Fishwick, Dr Frank (1992) *PA Book Trade Yearbook*, Publishers Association, 19 Bedford Square, London WC1 3HJ
* *Book Facts 1992*, Book Marketing Ltd, 7a Bedford Square, London WC1B 3RA
Books and the Consumer 1992, Book Marketing Ltd, 7a Bedford Square, London WC1B 3RA
Books as Gifts, Book Marketing Ltd, 7a Bedford Square, London WC1B 3RA
Books: The International Market 1992, Euromonitor, Dept W, 87-88 Turnmill St, London EC1M 5QU
Borrowing Books - Readership & Library Usage, Book Marketing Ltd, 7a Bedford Square, London WC1B 3RA
Bookselling in Britain 1992, Jordan & Sons Ltd, Freepost (BS2348), 21 St Thomas St, Bristol
Britain's Book Publishing Industry 1991, Jordan & Sons Ltd, Freepost (BS2348), 21 St Thomas St, Bristol
* *The Euromonitor Book Report 1991*, Euromonitor, Dept W, 87-88 Turnmill St, London EC1M 5QU
UK Publishing, Key Note Publs., Field House, 72 Oldfield Road, Hampton, Middx TW12 2HQ
World Book Markets 1992, Euromonitor, Dept W, 87-88 Turnmill St, London EC1M 5QU

Copyediting and Indexing:
Butcher, Judith (1992) *Copy-editing - The Cambridge Handbook*, 3rd edn,

Cambridge University Press
* Harris, Nicola (1991) *Basic Editing: a practical course*, Book House Training Centre/Unesco
Harts Rules for Compositors and Readers at the University Press, Oxford, 39th edn, (1983), Oxford University Press
* Knight, G Norman (1979) *Indexing, The Art of*, Allen & Unwin *Oxford Dictionary for Writers and Editors* (1981), Clarendon Press, Oxford

Copyright, Contracts & Rights
* *Copyright, Designs & Patents Act 1988*, HMSO
* Clark, Charles (1993) *Publishing Agreements: a book of precedents*, 4th edn, Butterworths
* Flint, Michael F (1985) *A User's Guide to Copyright*, 2nd edn, Butterworths
* Owen, Lynette (1991) *Selling Rights: a publisher's guide to success*, Blueprint (Chapman & Hall)
* Thorn, Eric A (1990) *Understanding Copyright : a practical guide*, Jay books
* *The Photographers' Guide to the 1988 Copyright Act* (1989) British Photographers' Liaison Committee, 9-10 Domingo St, London EC1

Design:
Martin, D (1989) *An Outline of Book Design*, Blueprint (Chapman & Hall)
* *Briefing Designers* (1992), Arts Council of Great Britain, 14 Great Peter Street, London SW1P 3NQ

Directories: (many of these are produced annually)
* *Directory of Booksellers Association Members*, The Booksellers Association of Great Britain & Ireland
* *Directory of Publishers & Wholesalers*, The Booksellers Association of Great Britain & Ireland
* *Directory of Publishing Vol. I* United Kingdom, Commonwealth and Overseas, *Vol. II* Continental Europe (1993), Cassell & The Publishers Association
The European Book World, Anderson Rand, The Scotts Bindery, Russell Court, Cambridge CB2 1HL
* *International Literary Market Place*, Bowker Saur, 60 Grosvenor St, London W1X 9DA
* *Literary Market Place*, Bowker Saur, 60 Grosvenor St, London W1X 9DA
* *Small Press Year Book*, Small Press Group of Britain Ltd, Publishers in the UK, Whitakers
* *The Education Authorities Directory and Annual*, School Govt. Publishing

Co., Darby House, Bletchingley Rd, Merstham, Redhill RH1 3DN
* *The Primary Education Directory*, School Govt.Publishing Co., Darby House, Bletchingley Rd, Merstham, Redhill RH1 3DN
The Libraries Directory 1991-93, James Clarke & Co, PO Box 60, Cambridge CB1 2NT
* Harrold, Ann (Ed) (1991) *Libraries in the United Kingdom and the Republic of Ireland*, Library Association Publishing Ltd
* *Scottish Library & Information Resources* (1991), Scottish Library Association
World Guide to Libraries, Bowker Saur, 60 Grosvenor St, London W1X 9DA
Directory of Information Sources in the United Kingdom, Aslib, Information House, 20-24 Old Street, London EC1V 9AP

DTP:
Cookman, Brian (1990) *Desktop Design: getting the professional look*, Blueprint (Chapman & Hall)
* Dorner, Jane (1992) *Writing on Disk*, John Taylor Book Ventures
* Hewson, David (1989) *Introduction to Desktop Publishing*, John Taylor Book Ventures
* Miles, John (1987) *Design for Desktop Publishing*, John Taylor Book Ventures
* Taylor, John and Heale, Shirley (1992) *Editing for Desktop Publishing*, John Taylor Book Ventures
Wilson-Davies, Kirty et al, Rev. Strutt, Ron (1991) *Desktop Publishing*, 4th edn, Blueprint (Chapman & Hall)

Freelancers:
* *The Directory of Publishing in Scotland*, Scottish Publishers Association
* *Indexers Available*, The Society of Indexers
* *The National Union of Journalists Freelance Directory*, Acorn House, 314 Gray's Inn Road, London WC1X 8DP
* *The National Union of Journalists Freelance Fees Guide*, Acorn House, 314 Gray's Inn Road, London WC1X 8DP
* *The Society of Freelance Editors and Proofreaders Directory*

Grants & Prizes:
* *Guide to Literary Prizes, Grants & Awards*, Book Trust, 45 East Hill, London SW18 2QZ
The Arts Funding Guide, Directory of Social Change, Radius Works, Back Lane, London NW3 1HL

Negotiation:
* Kennedy, Gavin (1992) *The Perfect Negotiation*, Century Business
* Rose, Colin (1989) *Negotiate and Win*, SPA Books

Picture Research:
Evans, Hilary & Mary (1992) *Picture Researcher's Handbook*, 5th edn, Blueprint (Chapman & Hall)
Evans, Hilary (1992) *Practical Picture Research*, Blueprint (Chapman & Hall)

Publicity & Marketing:
* Baverstock, Alison (1992) *How to Market Books*, Kogan Page Ltd
Bodian, Nat G (1980) *Book Marketing Handbook-Tips and Techniques*, Bowker Saur
Bodian, Nat G (1983) *Book Marketing Handbook, Volume 2 - Over 1000 More Tips and Techniques*, Bowker Saur
* Dickinson, Sarah (1990) *How to take on the Media*, Weidenfeld & Nicolson
Author Events - Impact and Effectiveness, Book Marketing Ltd, 7a Bedford Square, London WC1B 3RA
* *Book Promotion, Sales and Distribution: a management training course* (1991), Book House Training Centre/Unesco
Benn's Media Directory UK/Europe/World, Benn Business Info, PO Box 20, Sovereign Way, Tonbridge, Kent TN9 1RQ
BRAD - Media Facts at your Fingertips, Maclean Hunter Ltd, Maclean Hunter House, Chalk Lane, Cockfosters Rd, Barnet, Herts EN4 0BU
Hollis Press & Public Relations Annual, Hollis, Contact House, Lower Hampton Rd, Sunbury on Thames, Middx TW16 5HG
* *PIMS UK Media Directory*, PIMS UK Ltd, PIMS House, Mildmay Avenue, London N1 4RS
* *Willings Press Guide*, Reed Information Services, Windsor Court, East Grinstead House, East Grinstead, West Sussex RH19 1XA

Publishing- general:
Bingley, C (1972) *The Business of Book Publishing*, Pergamon
* Clark, Giles N (1988) *Inside Book Publishing: a career builder's guide*, Blueprint (Chapman & Hall)
* Collin, P H (1989) *Dictionary of Printing and Publishing*, Peter Collin Publishing Ltd
Curwen, Peter J (1981) *The UK Publishing Industry*, Pergamon
Norrie, Ian (1982) *Mumby's Publishing and Bookselling in the Twentieth*

Century, 6th edn, Bell & Hyman
* Ward, Audrey and Philip (1979) *The Small Publisher*, Oleander

Writers:
Barnard, Michael (1989)   *Making Electronic Manuscripts*, Blueprint (Chapman & Hall)
* Bell, Charlie (1991) *The Writers Guide to Self-publishing*,The Dragonfly Press
Bolt, David (1986) *The Author's Handbook*, Piatkus Books
Finch, Peter (1985) *How to Publish your Poetry*, Allison & Busby
Hyland, Paul (1992) *Getting Into Poetry*, Bloodaxe Books
Legat, Michael (1986) *Writing for Pleasure and Profit*, Robert Hale
* Legat, Michael (1987) *The Authors Guide to Publishing*, Robert Hale
* Turner, Barry (annual) *The Writers Handbook*, Macmillan/PEN
Guide for Authors (1985) Basil Blackwell Ltd
UK Tax Guide for Authors, Ernst & Young, Becket House, 1 Lambeth Palace Rd, London SE1 7EU
* *The Writers & Artists Yearbook* (annual), A & C Black

Note:
* Books marked with an asterisk are in the SPA's resource library and available to SPA members only for consultation or loan on request. The library also contains trade magazines, including *Publishing News*, *The Bookseller* and the US *Publishers Weekly*.